VIKING
COLORING BOOK

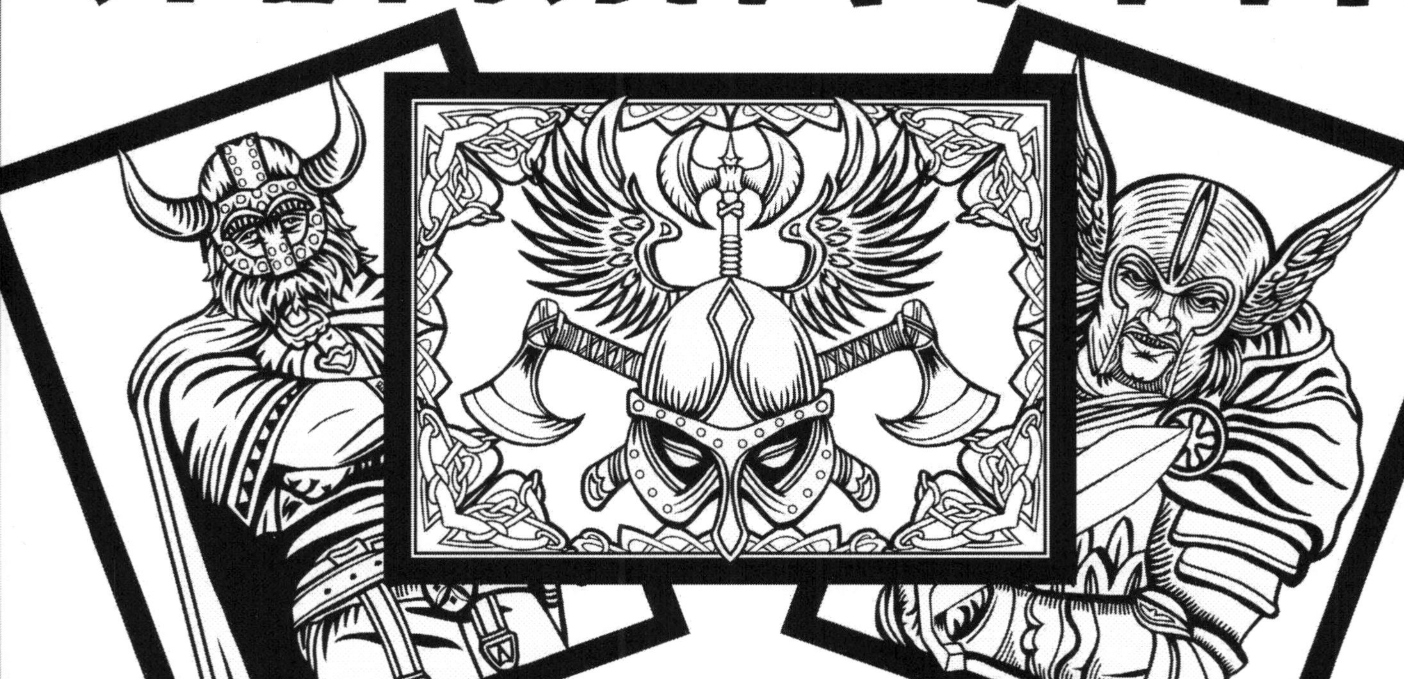

50

horizontal and vertical coloring pages

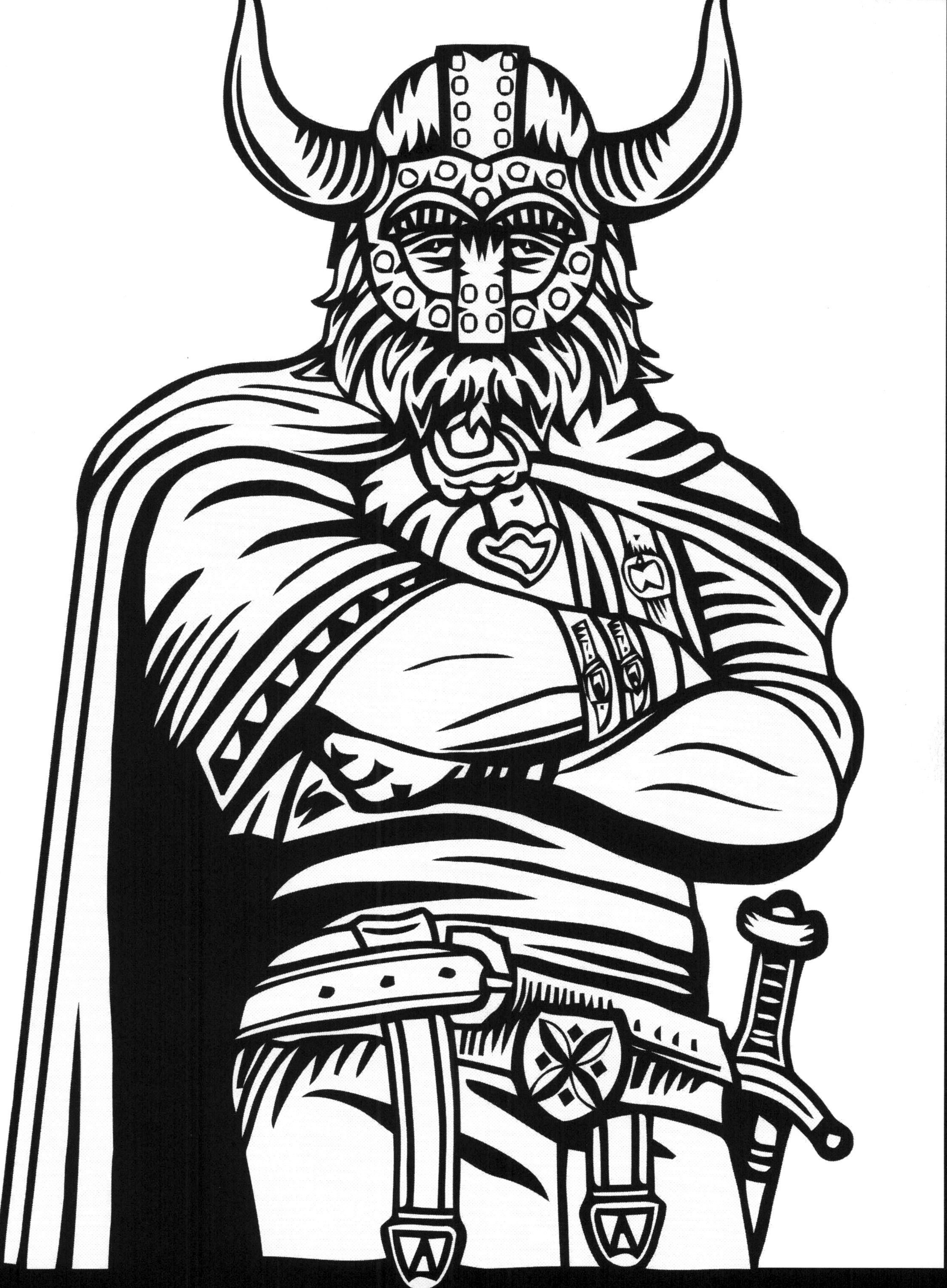

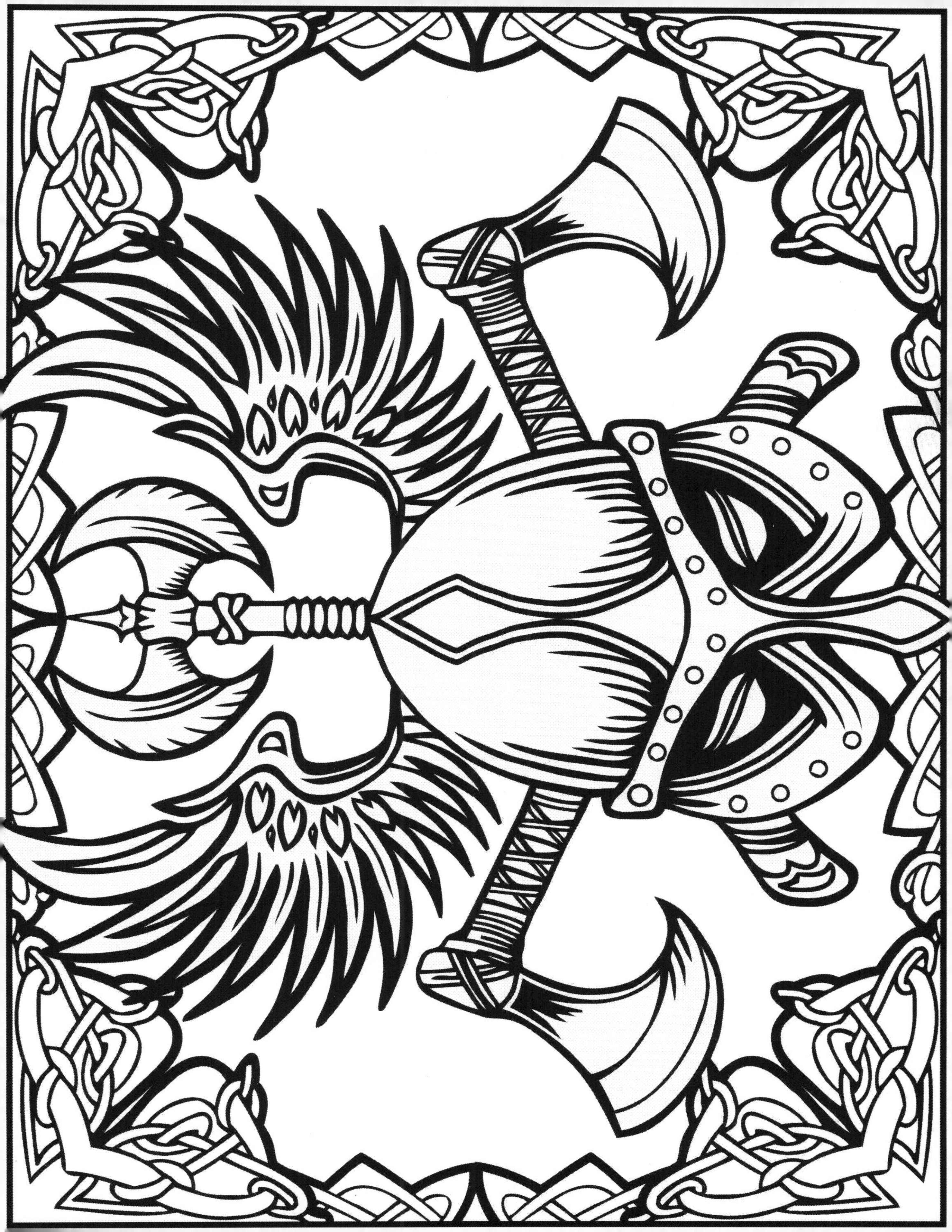

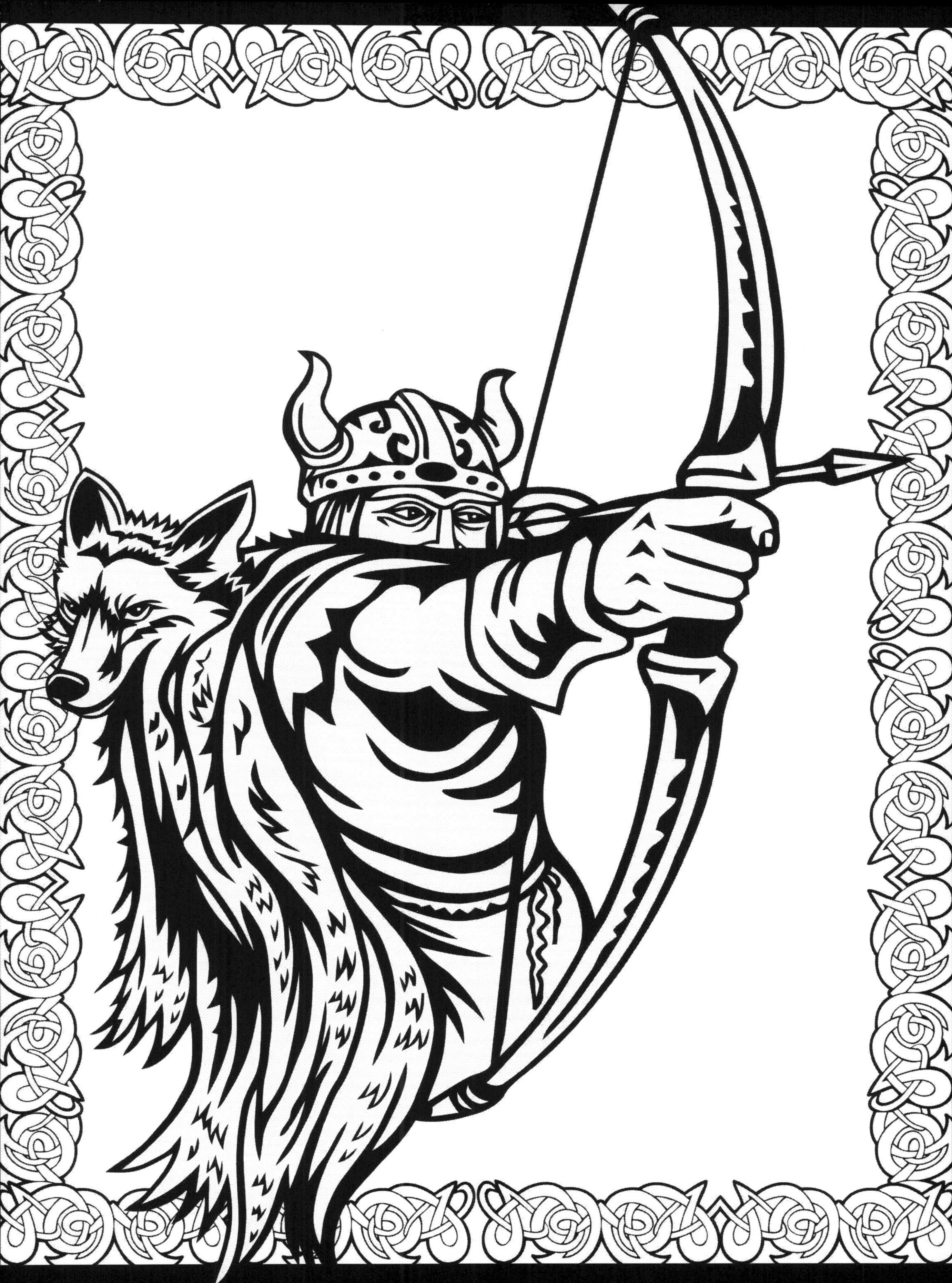

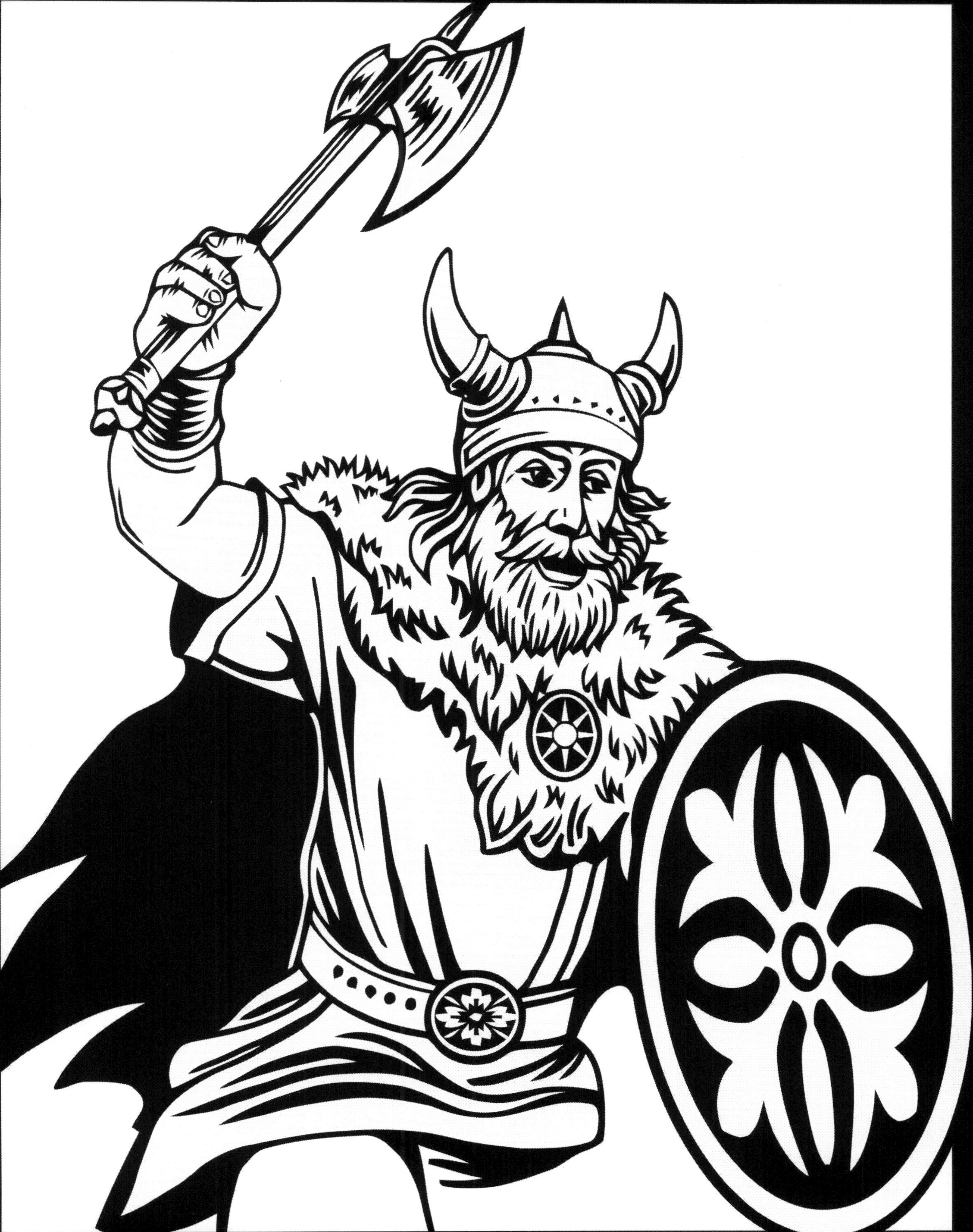

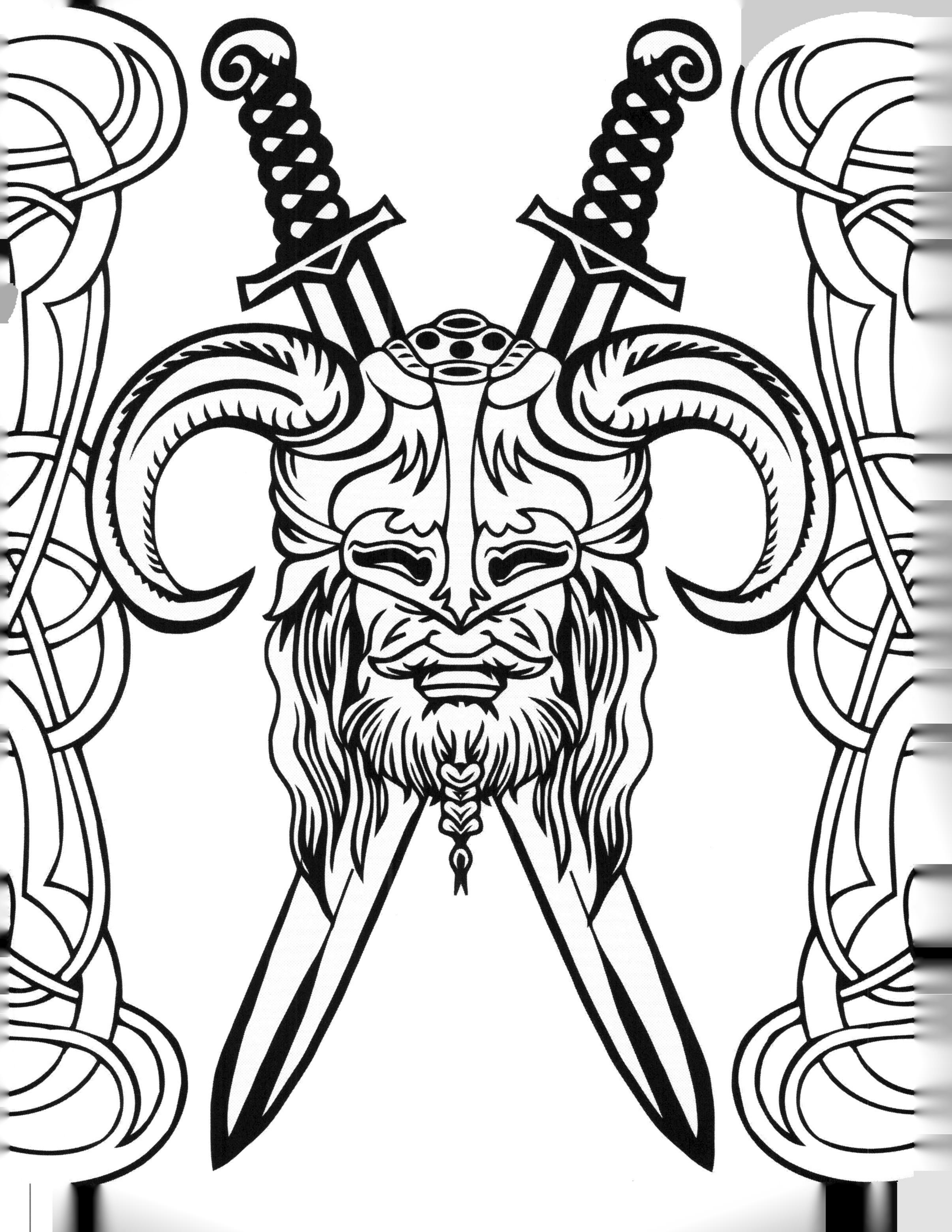

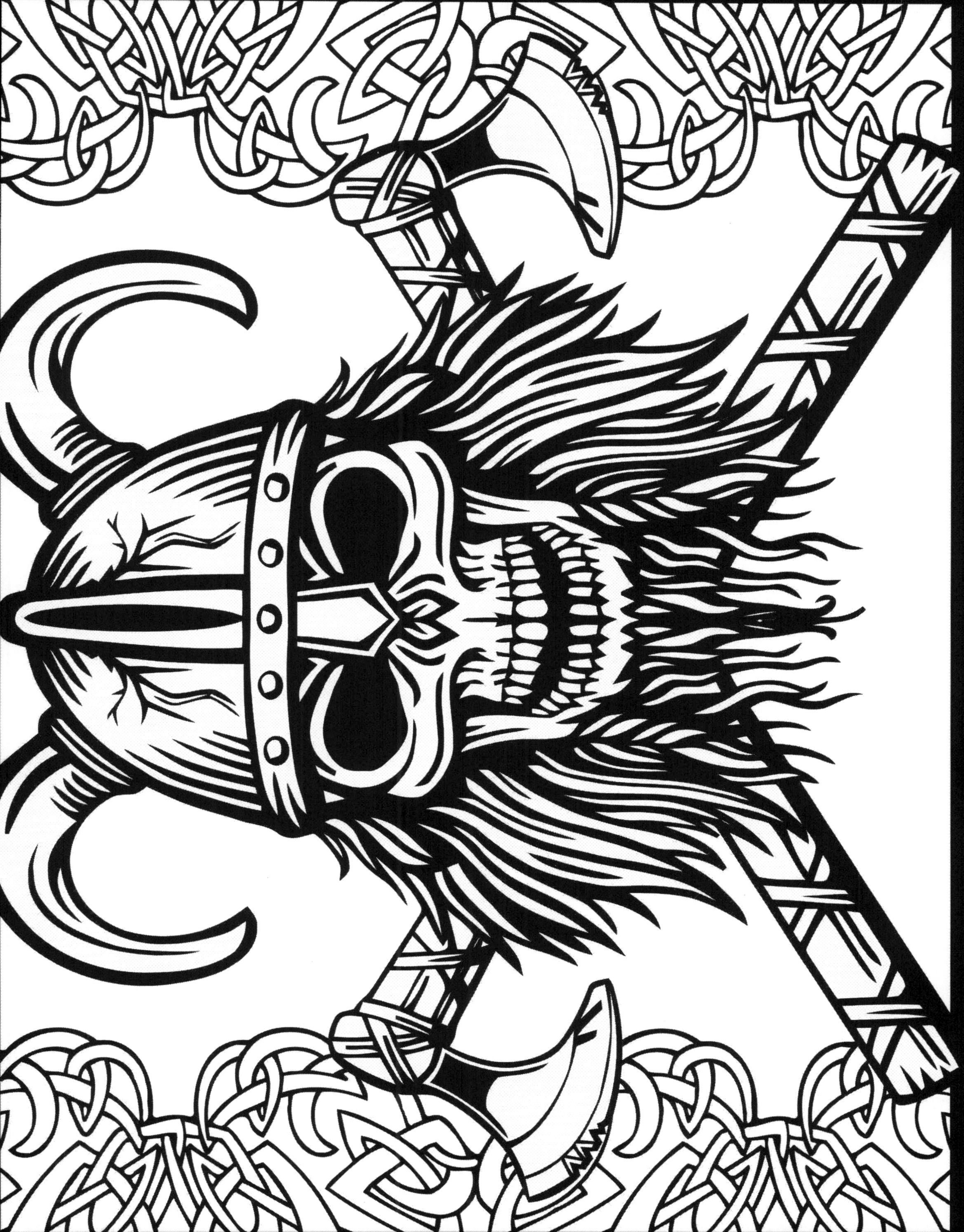

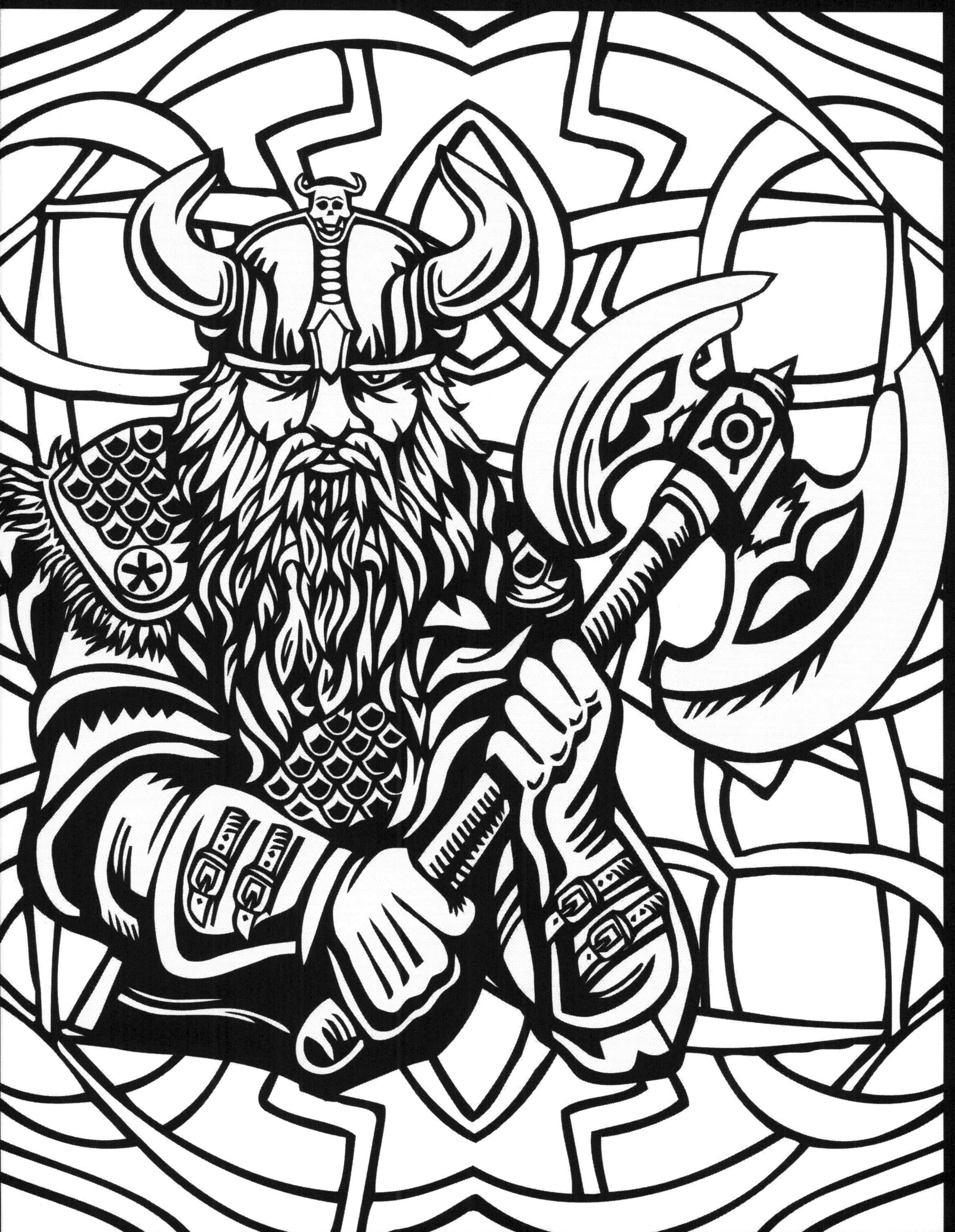

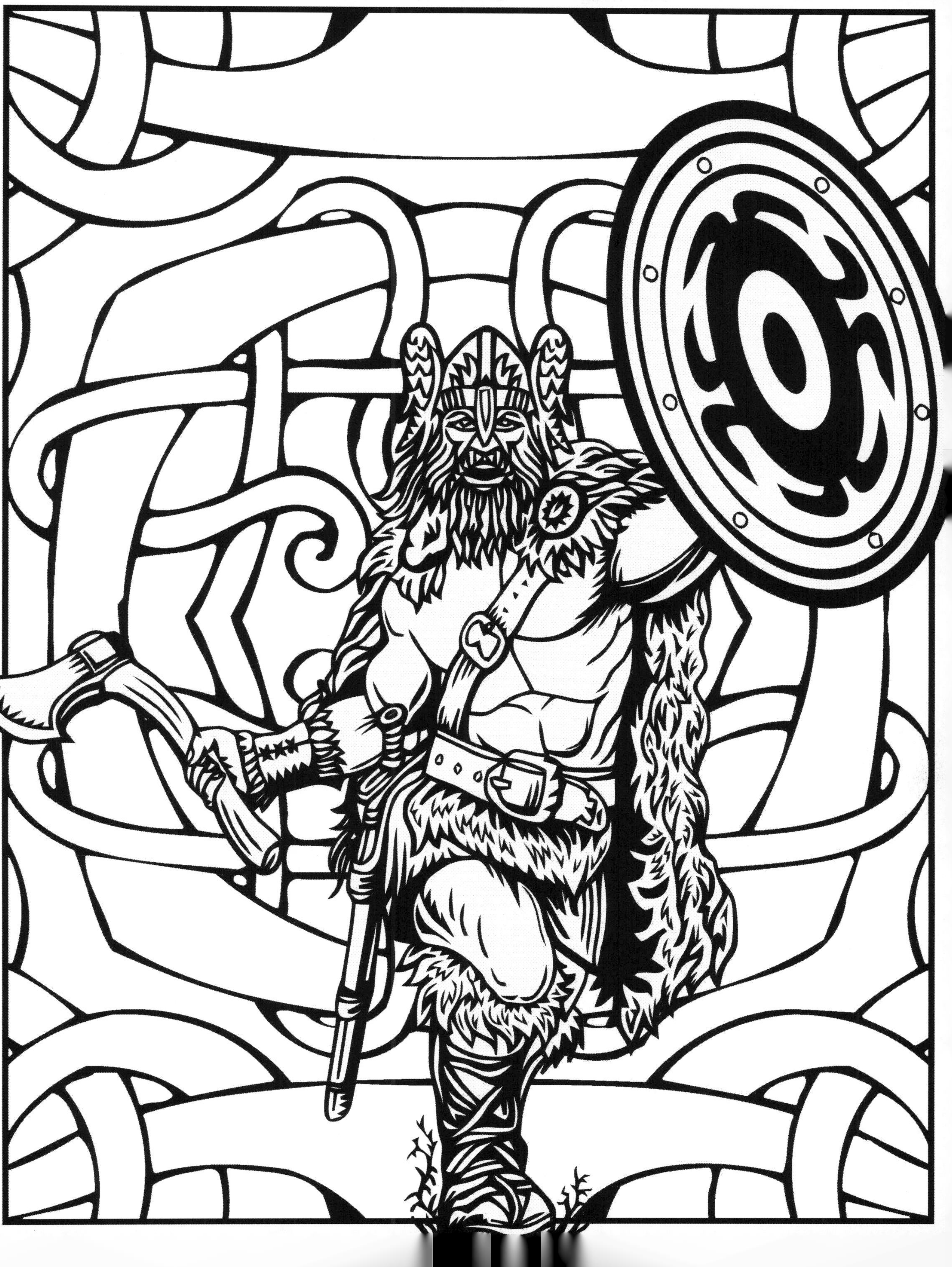

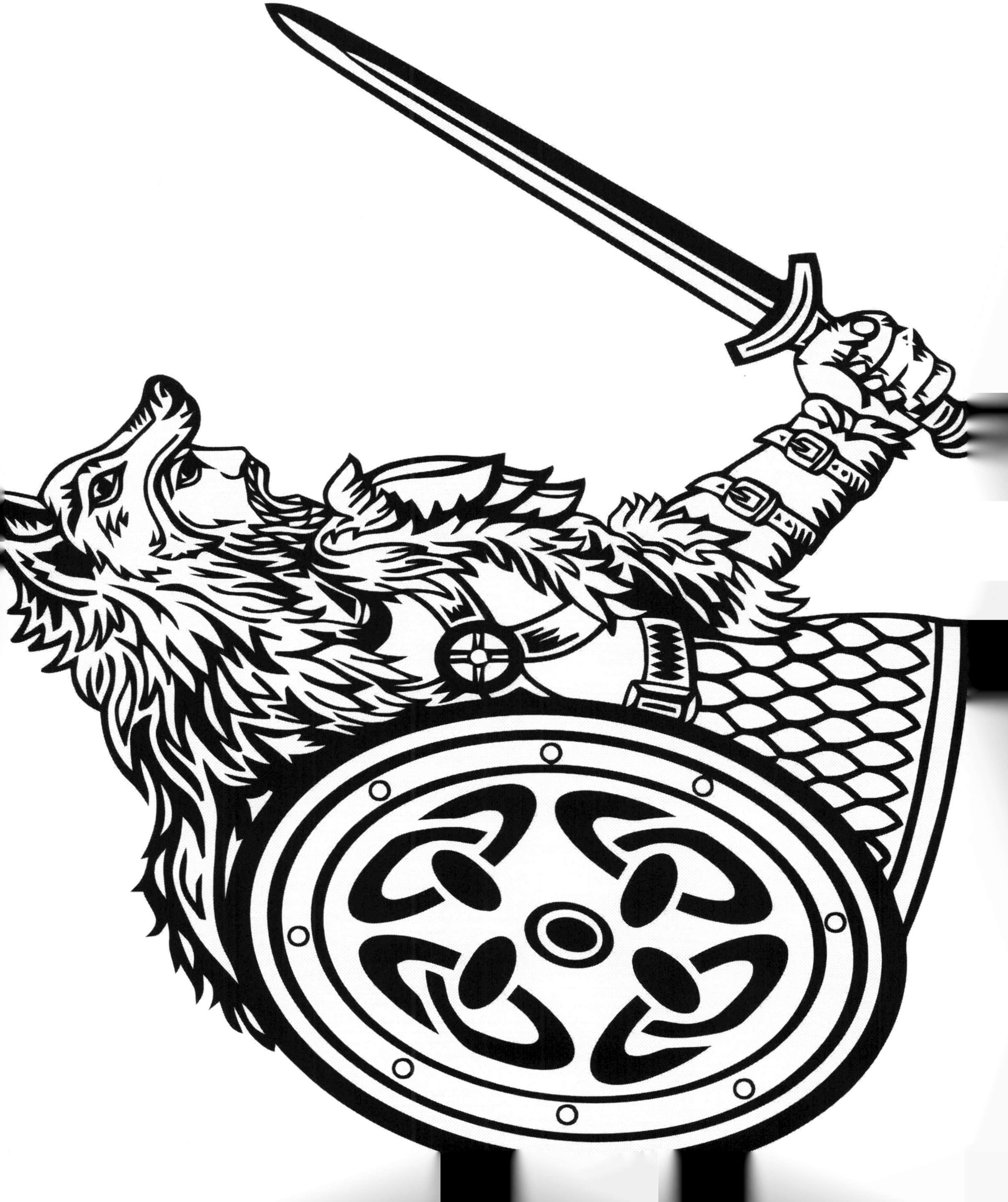

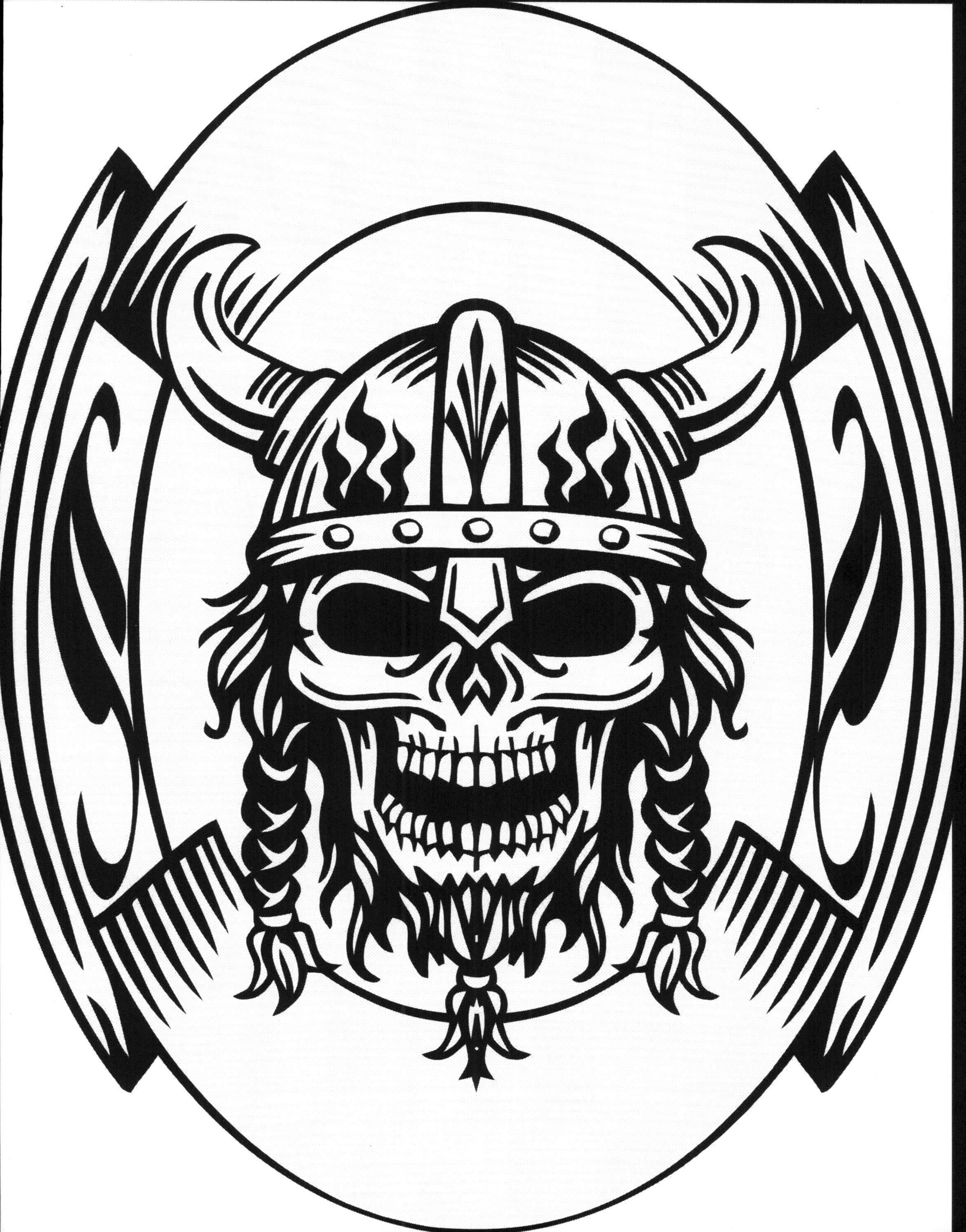

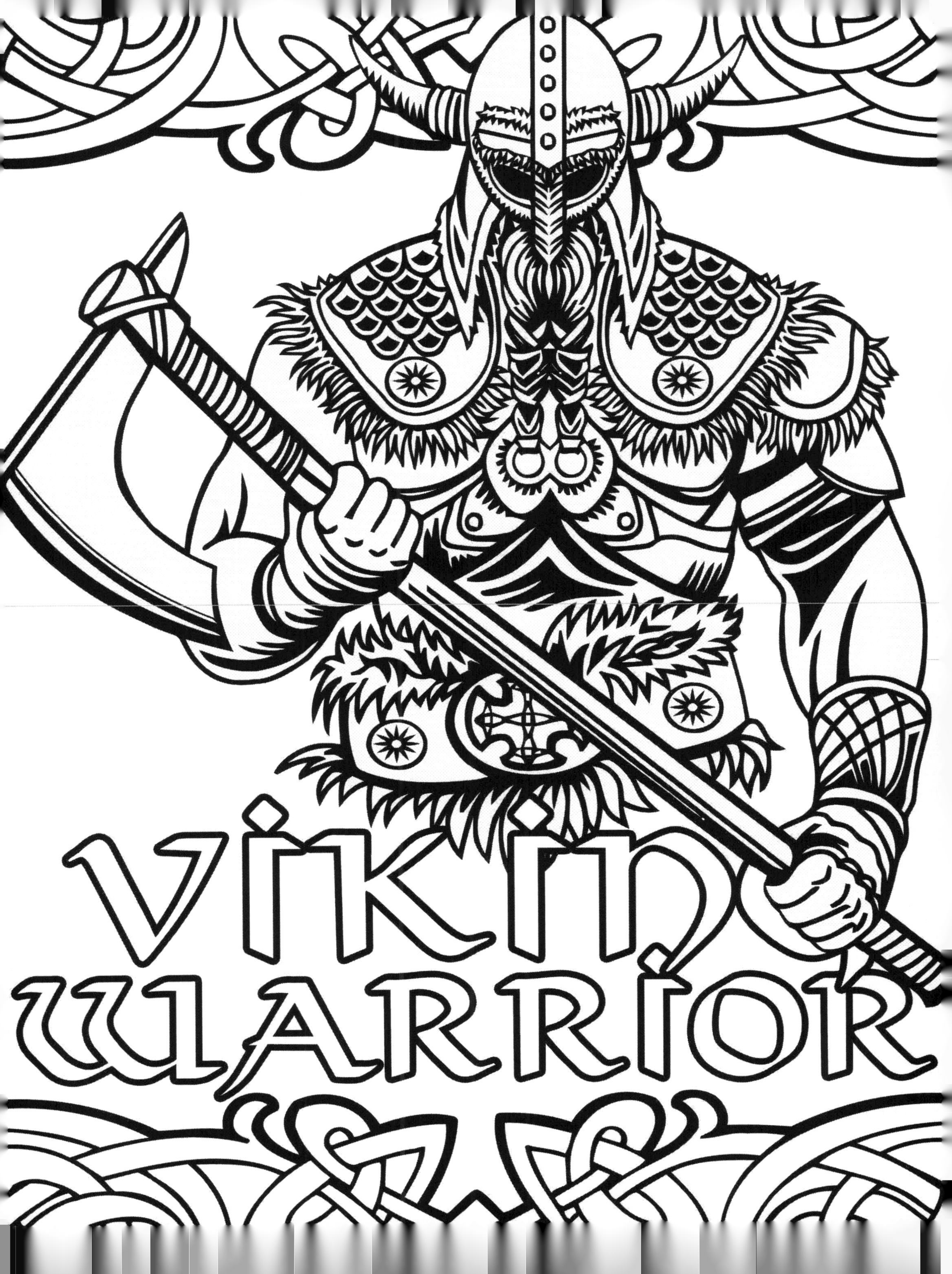
VIKIN
WARRIOR

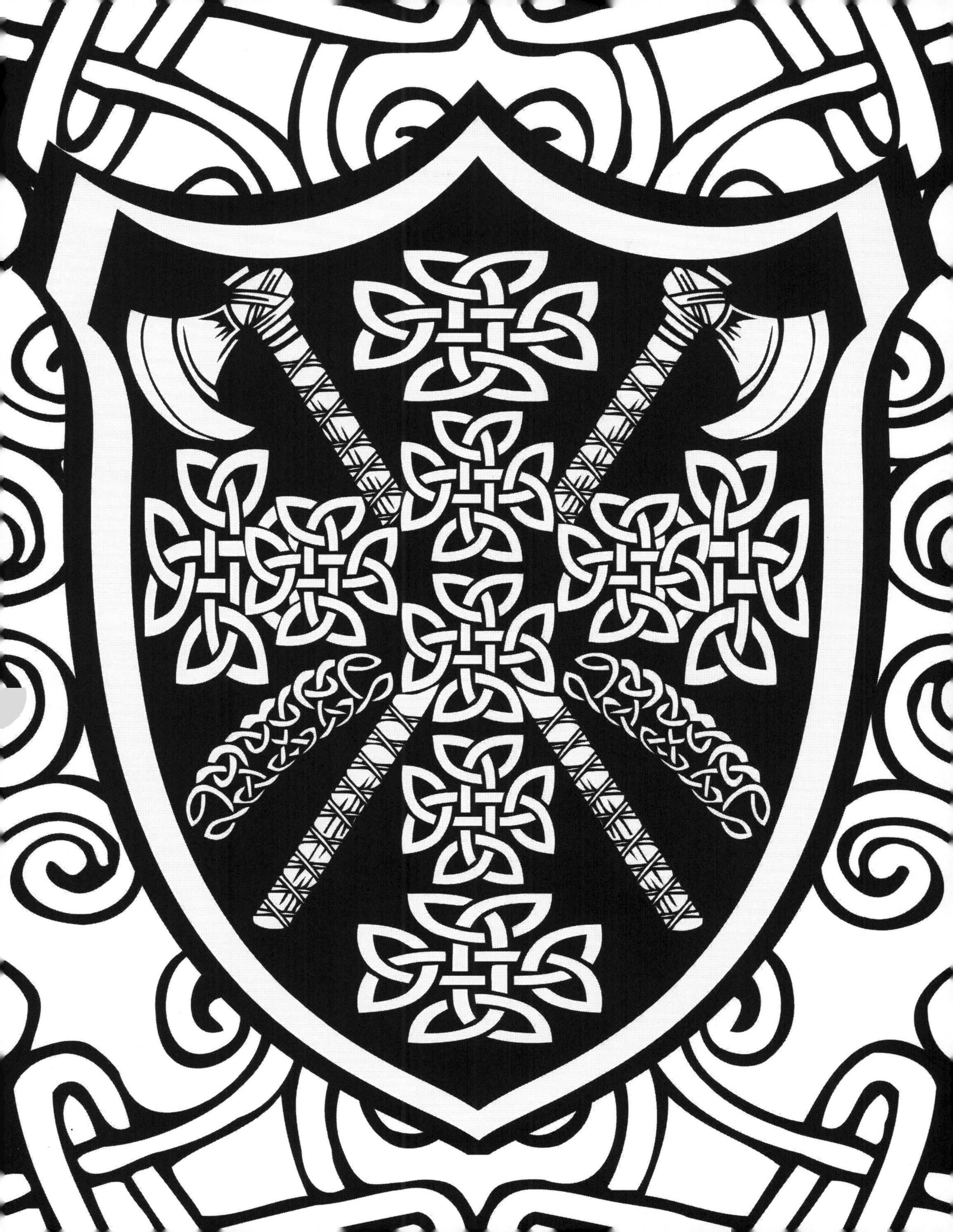

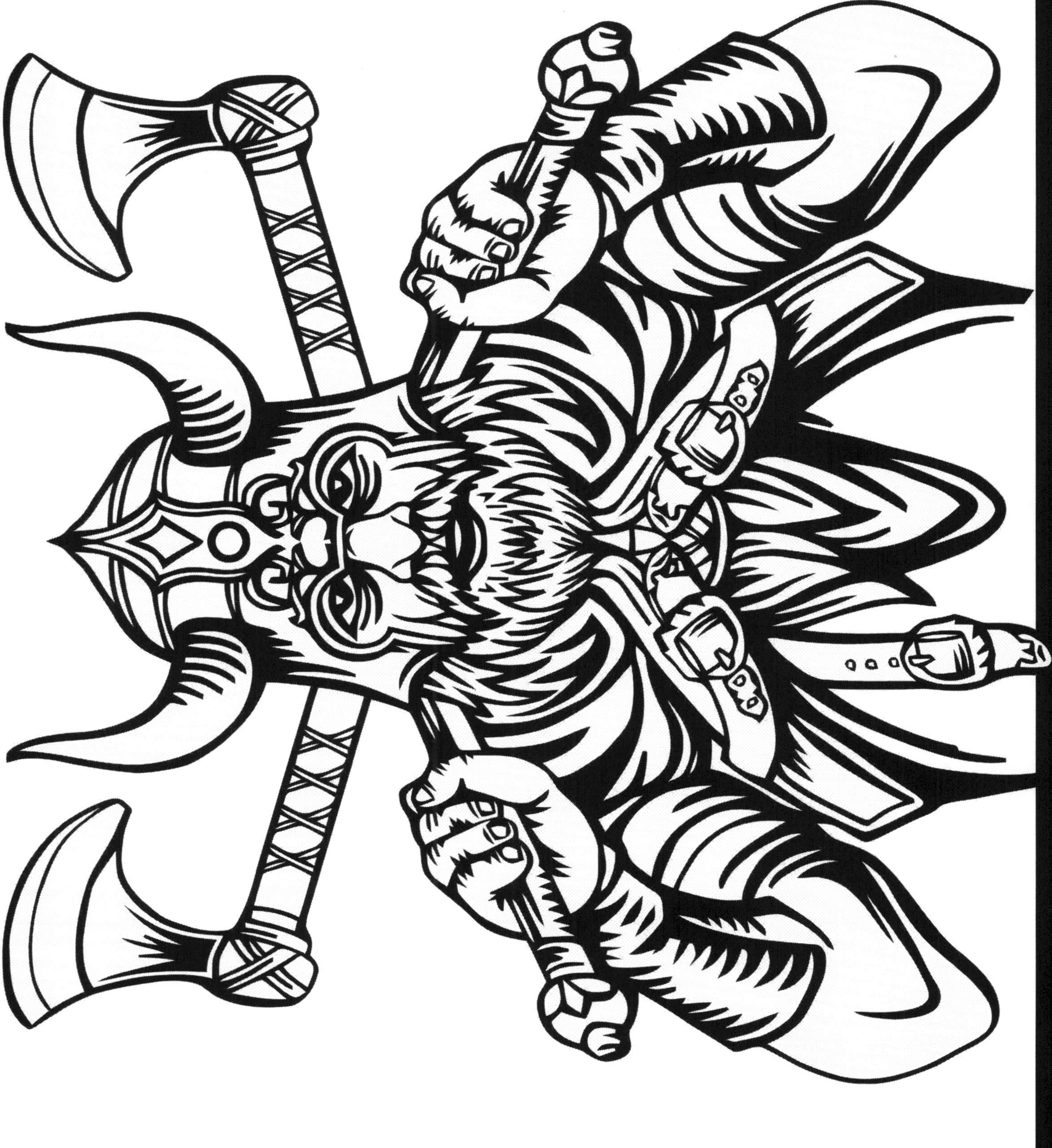

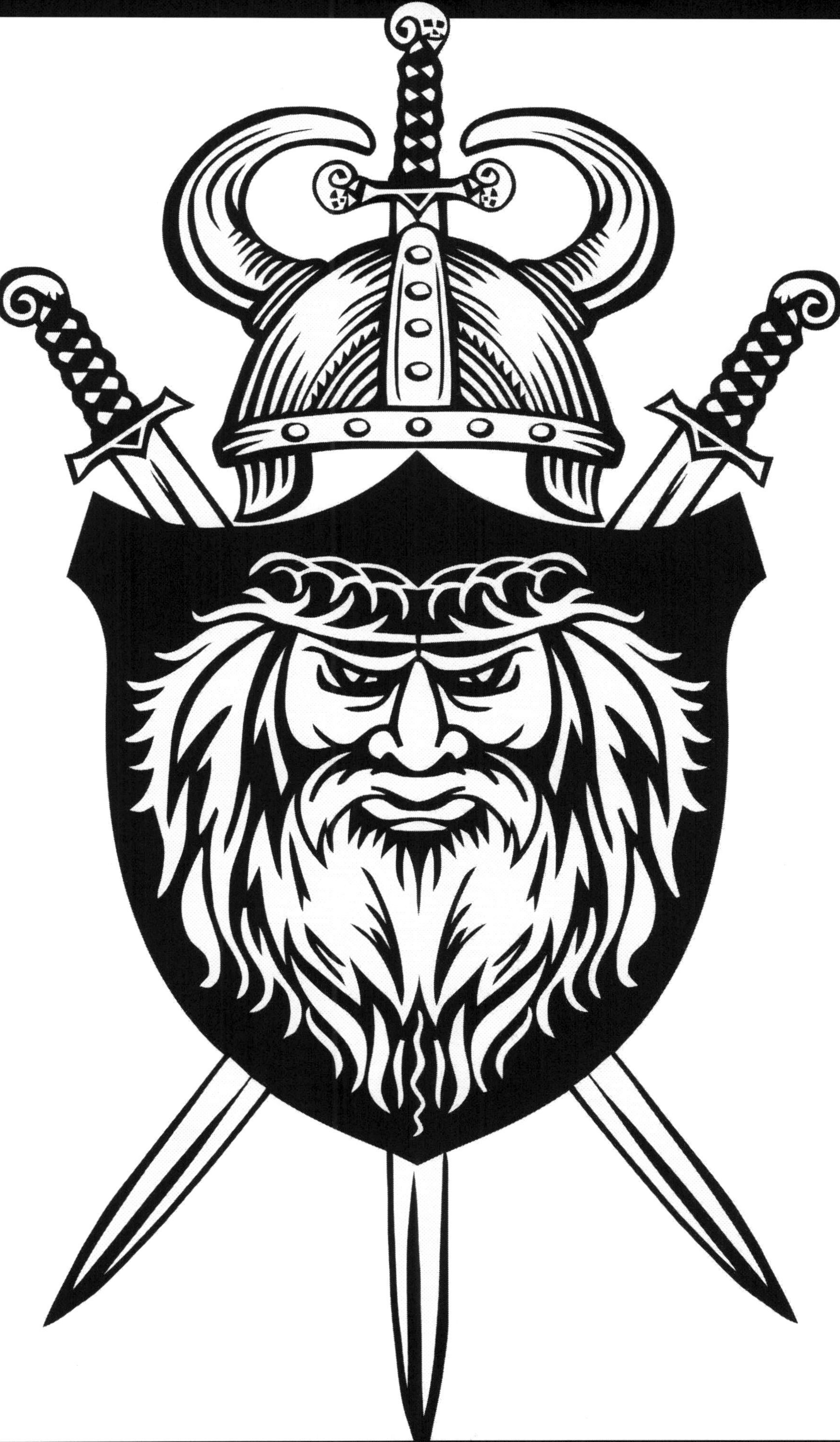

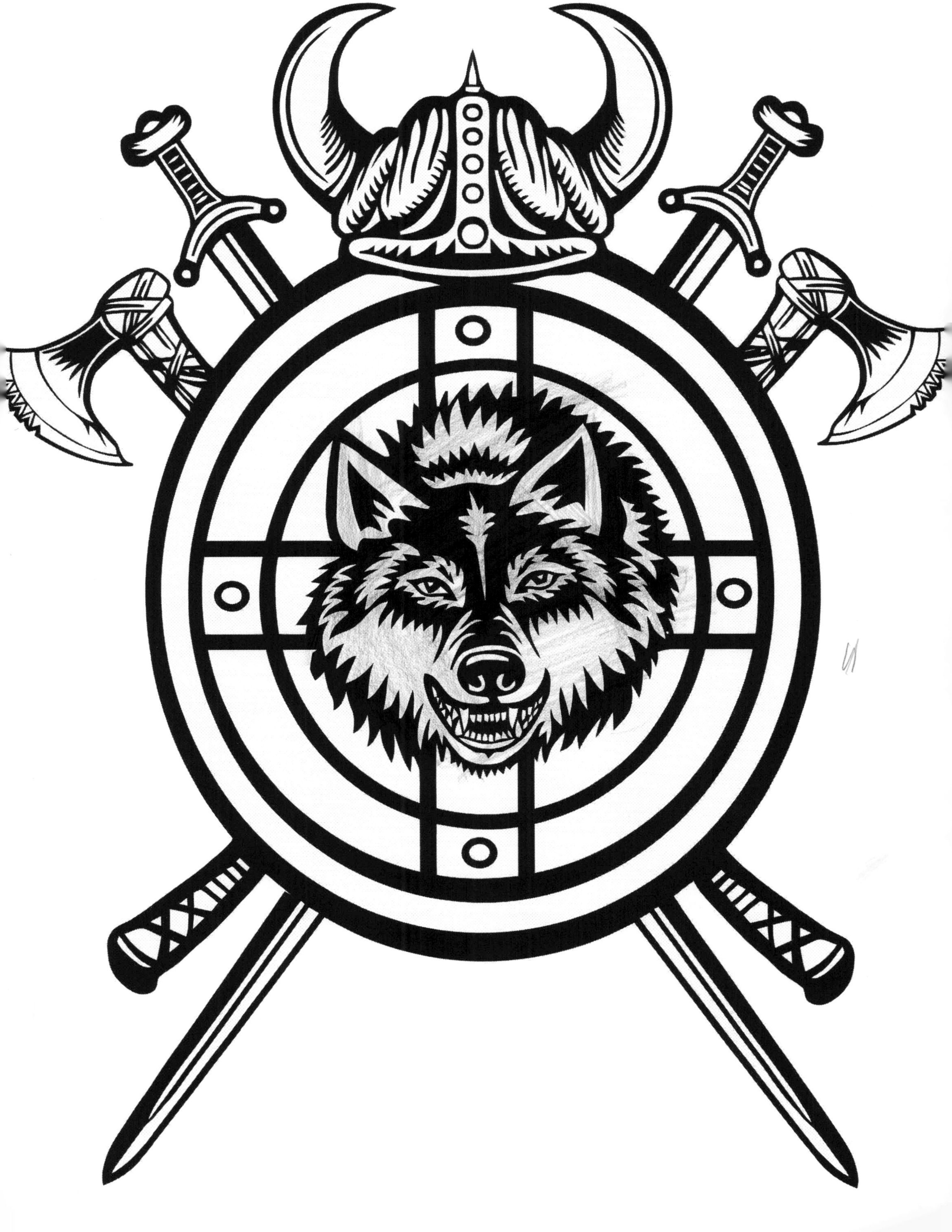

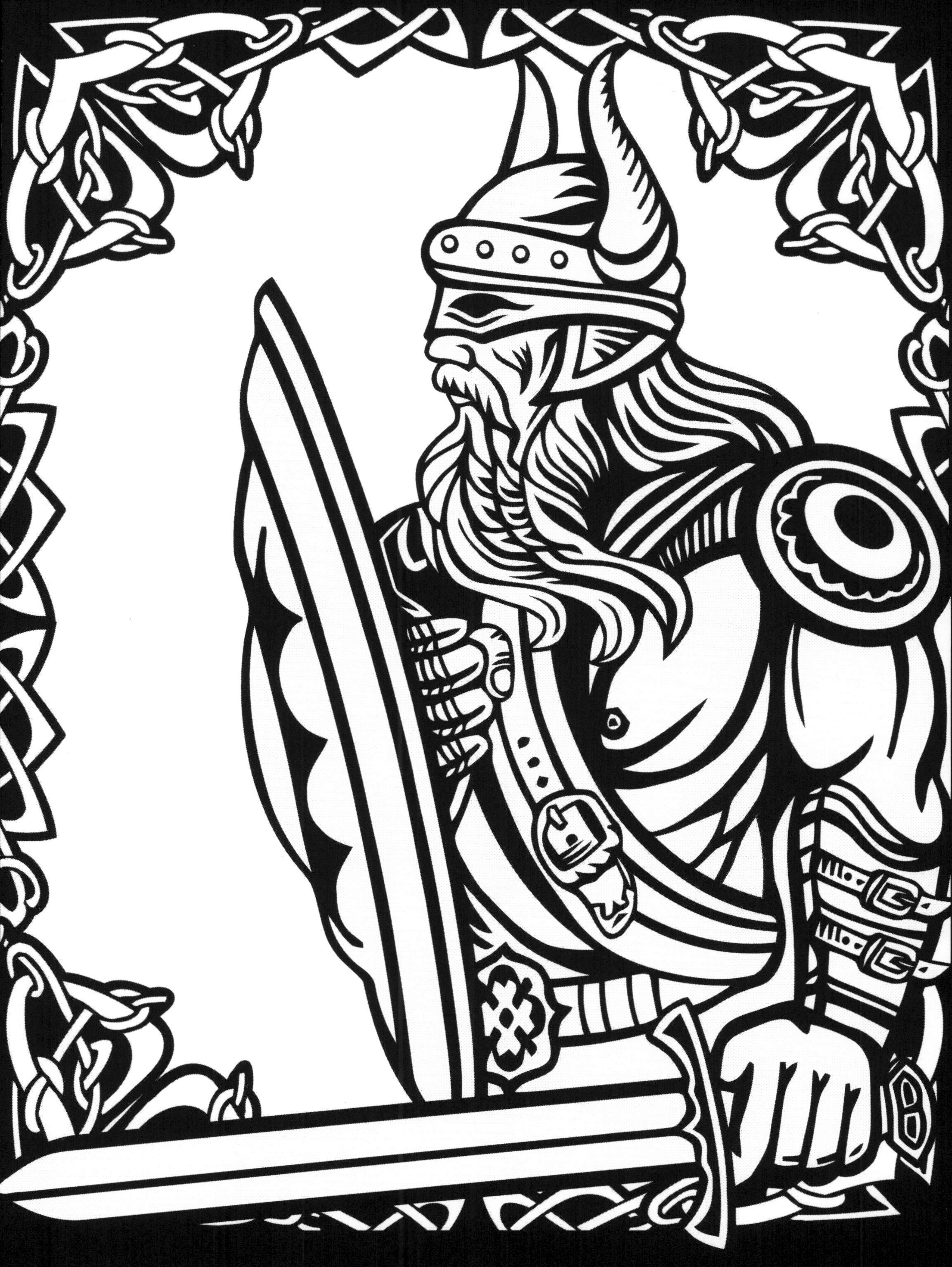

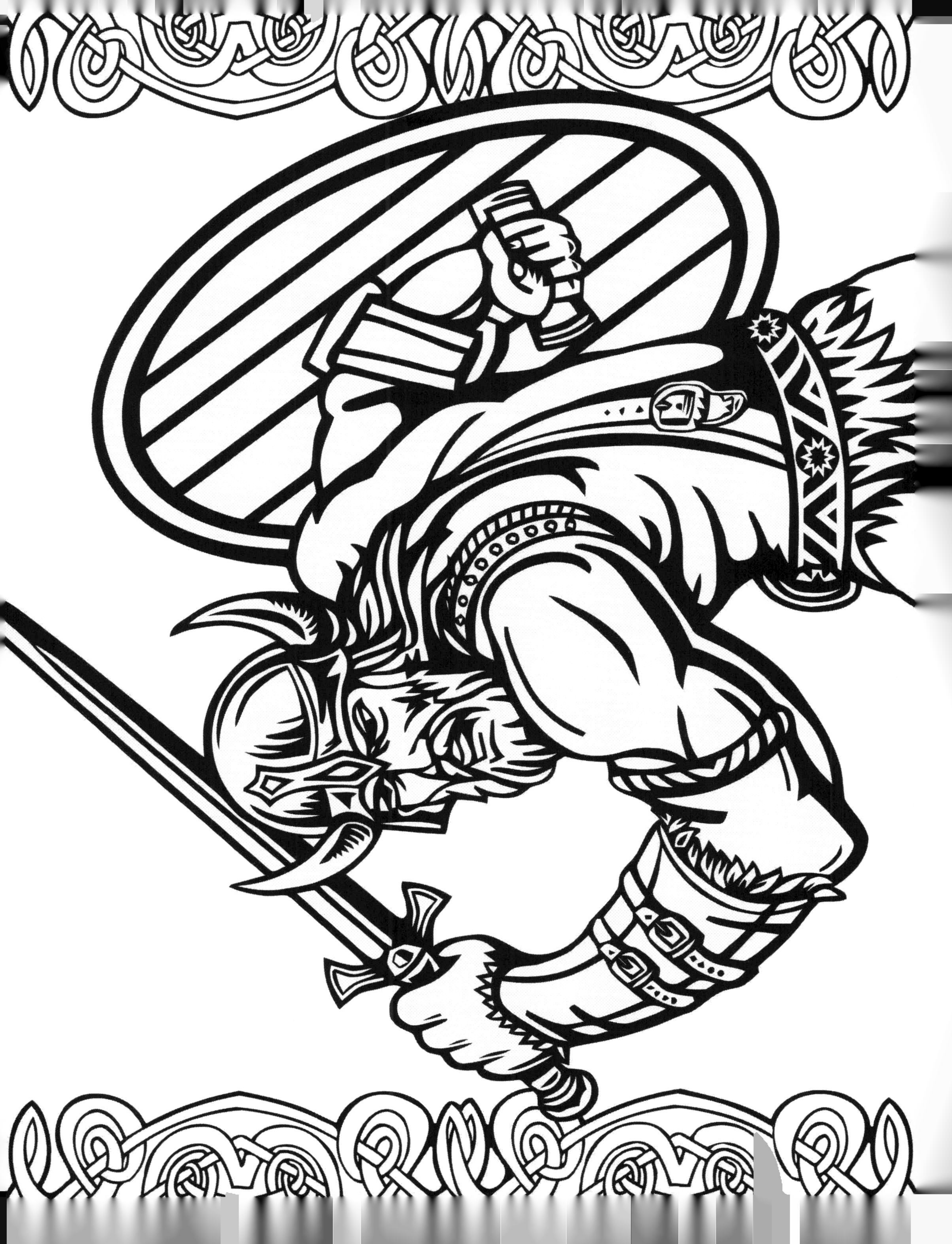

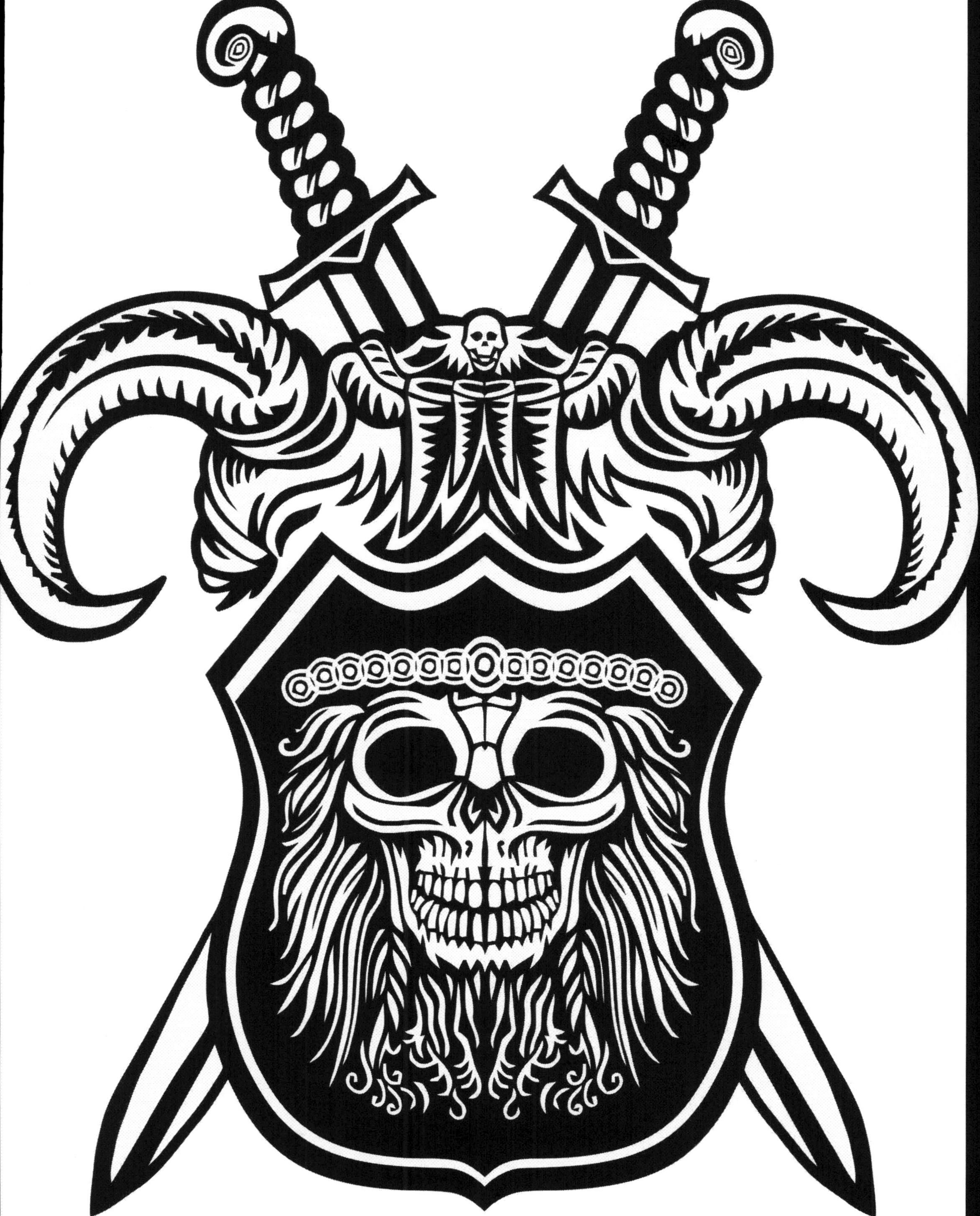

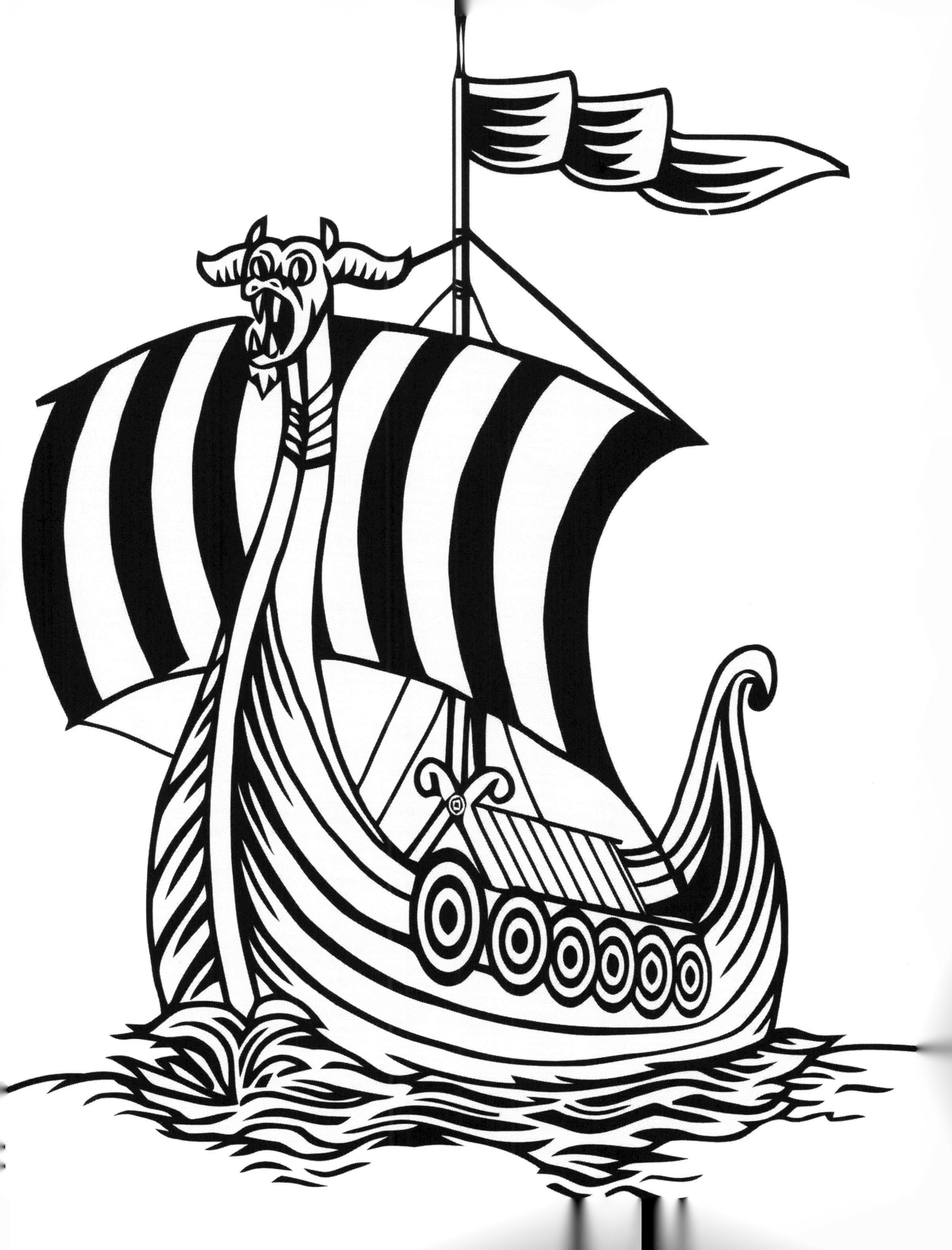

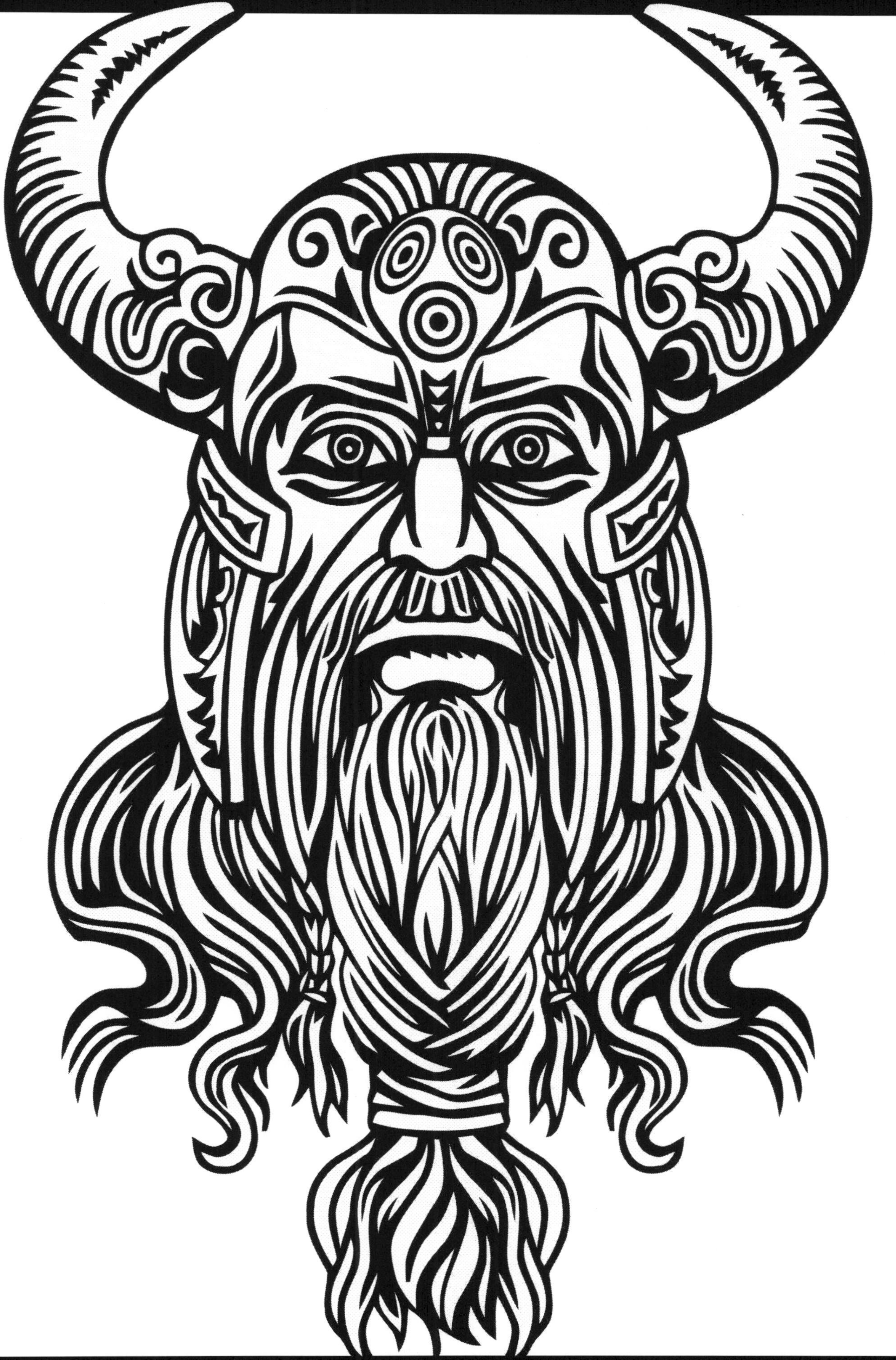

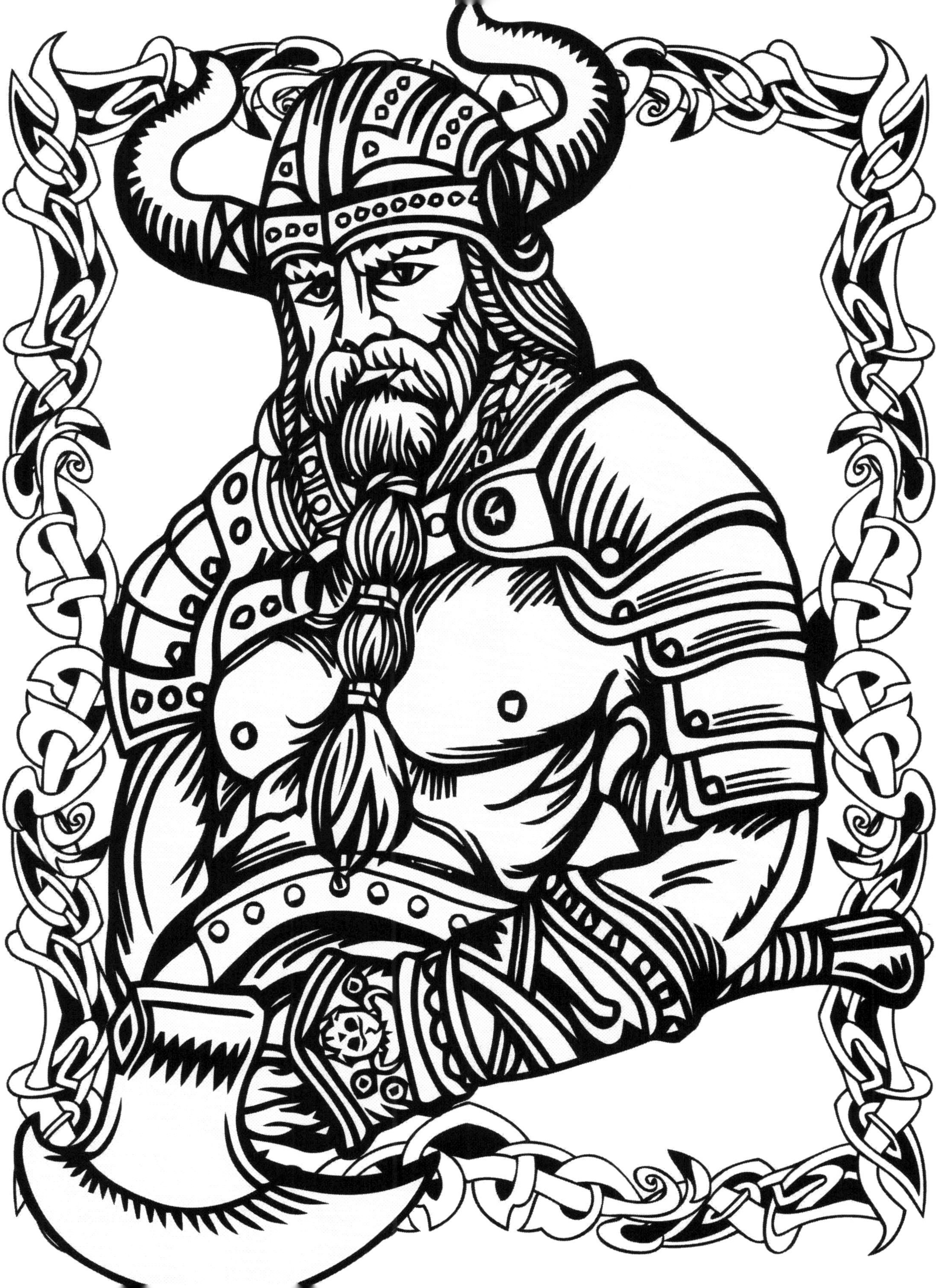

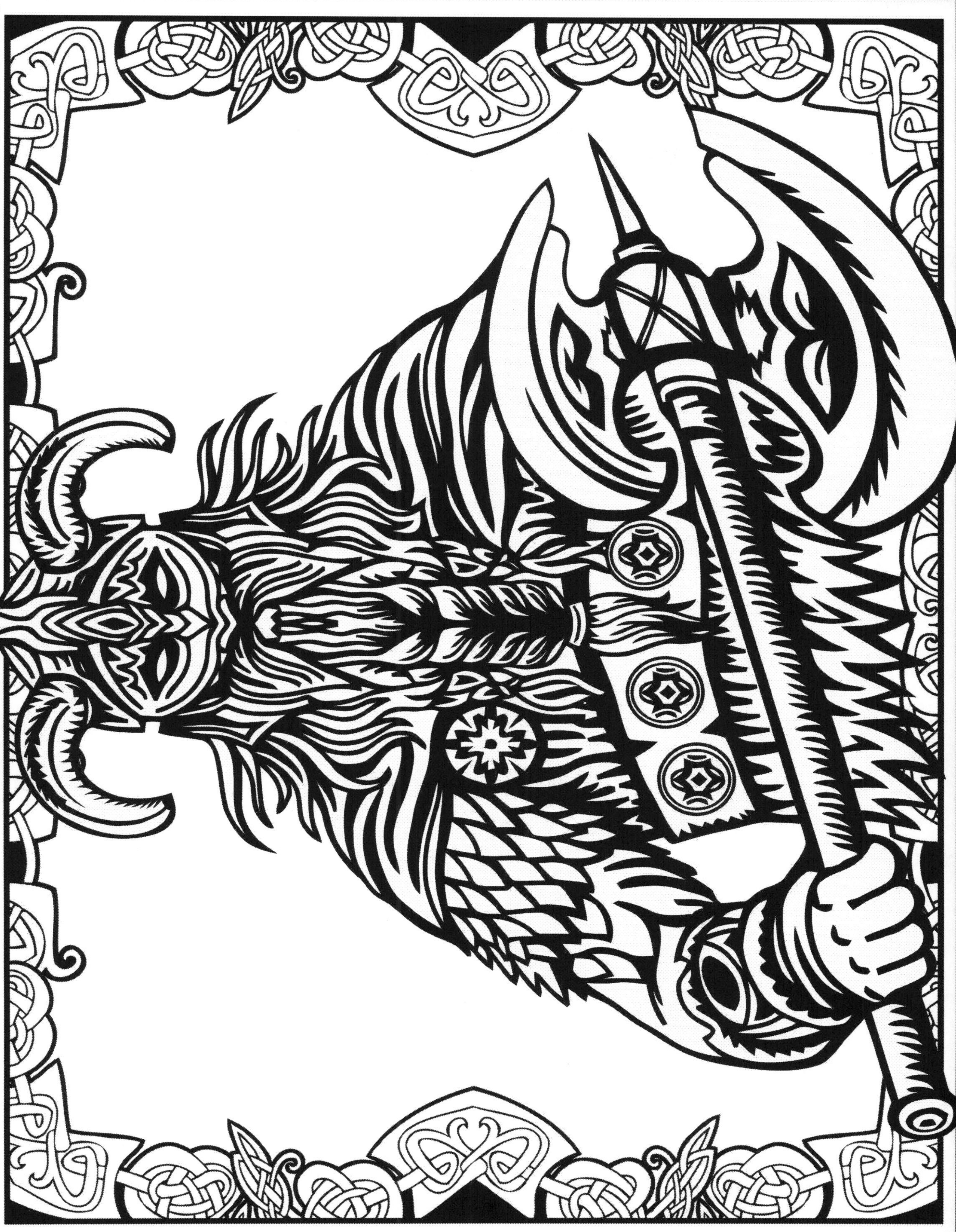

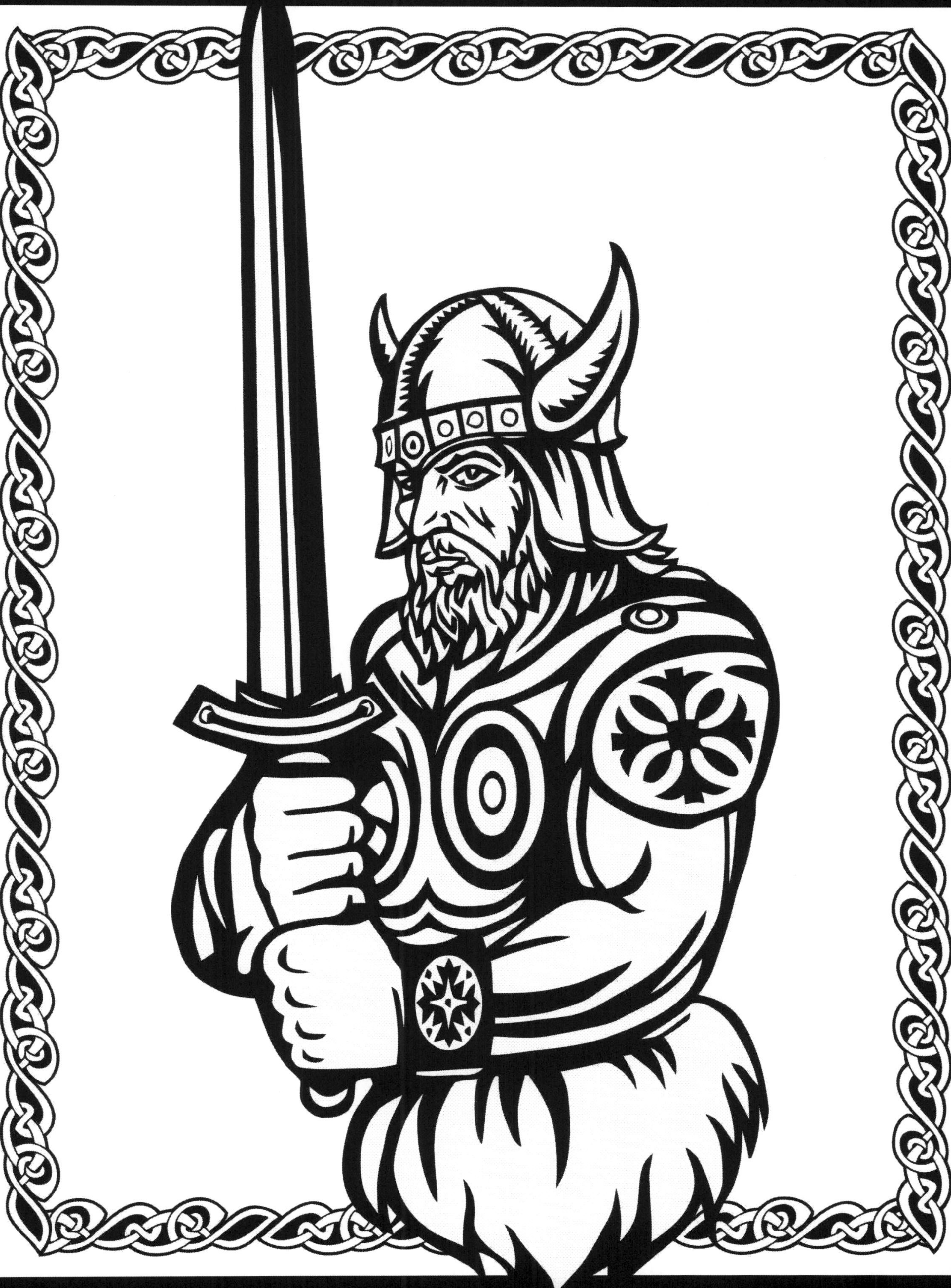

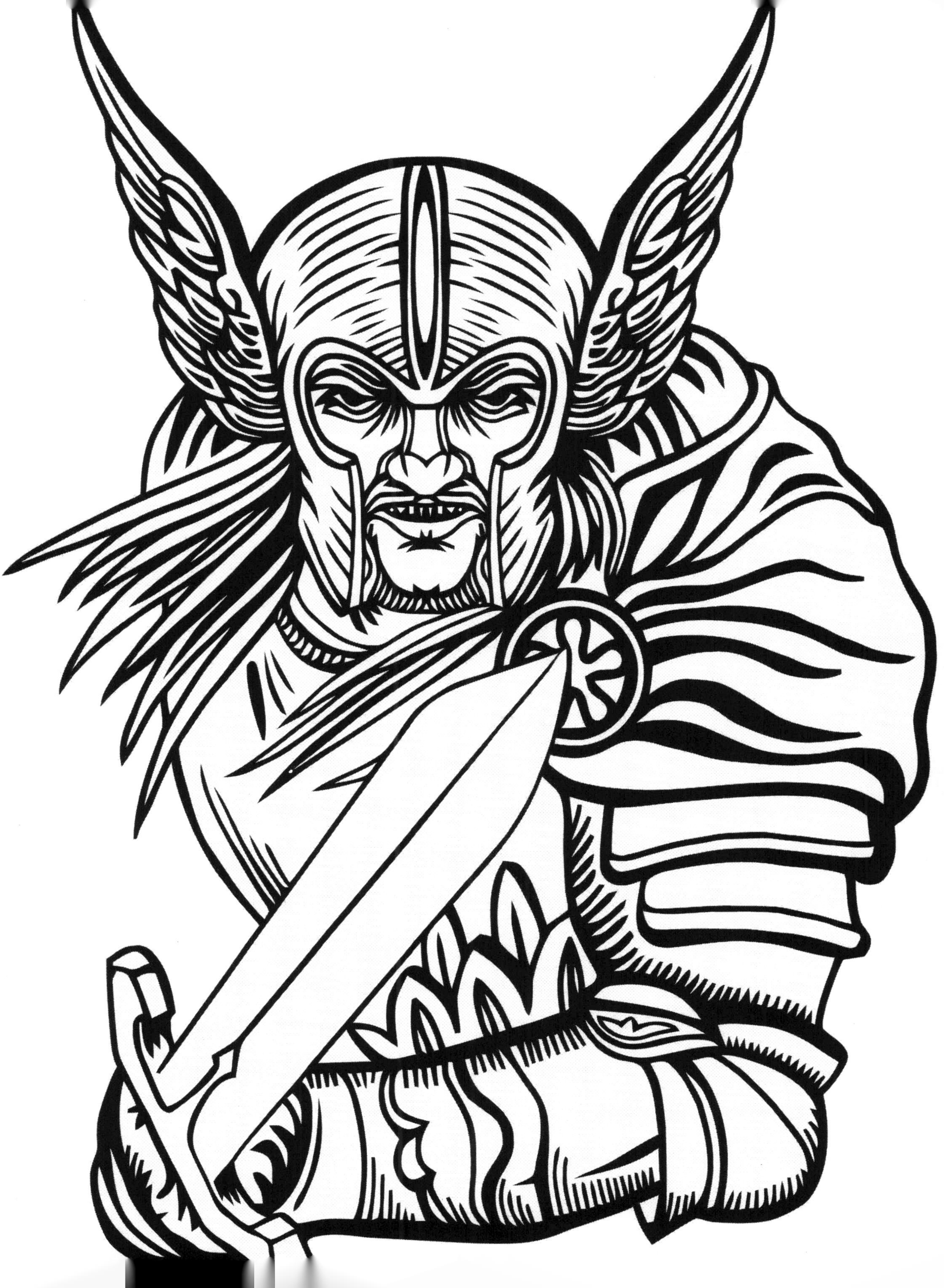

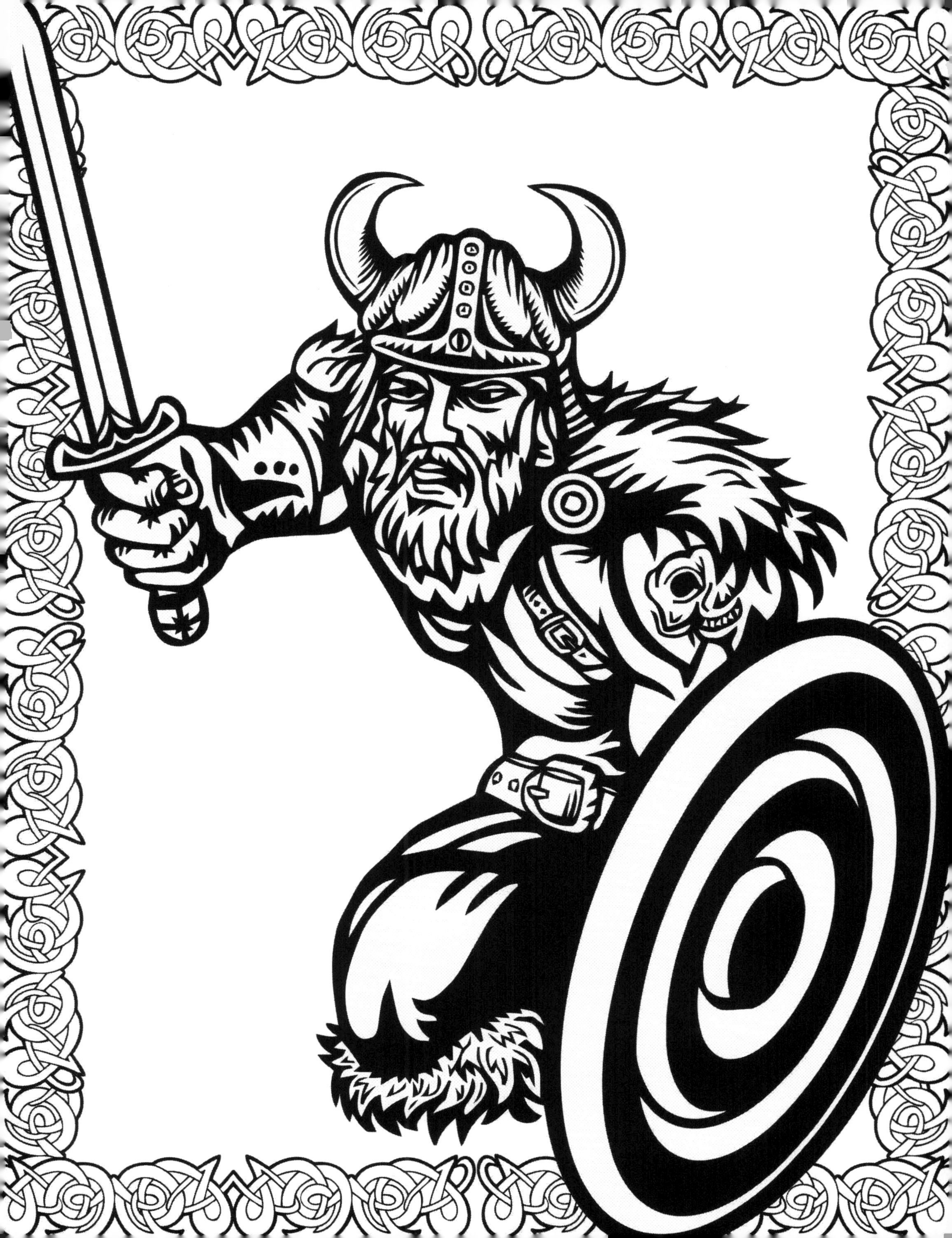

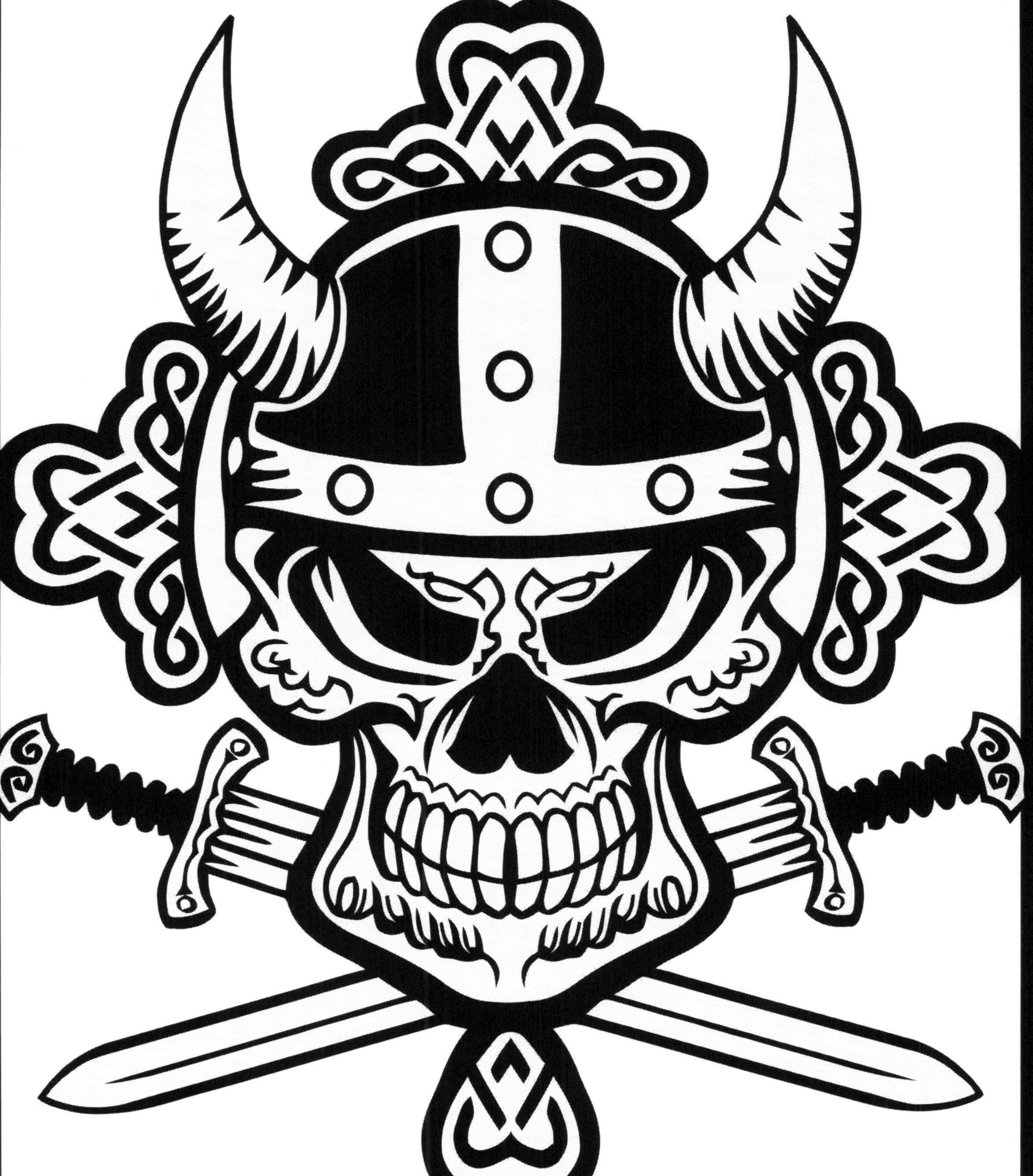

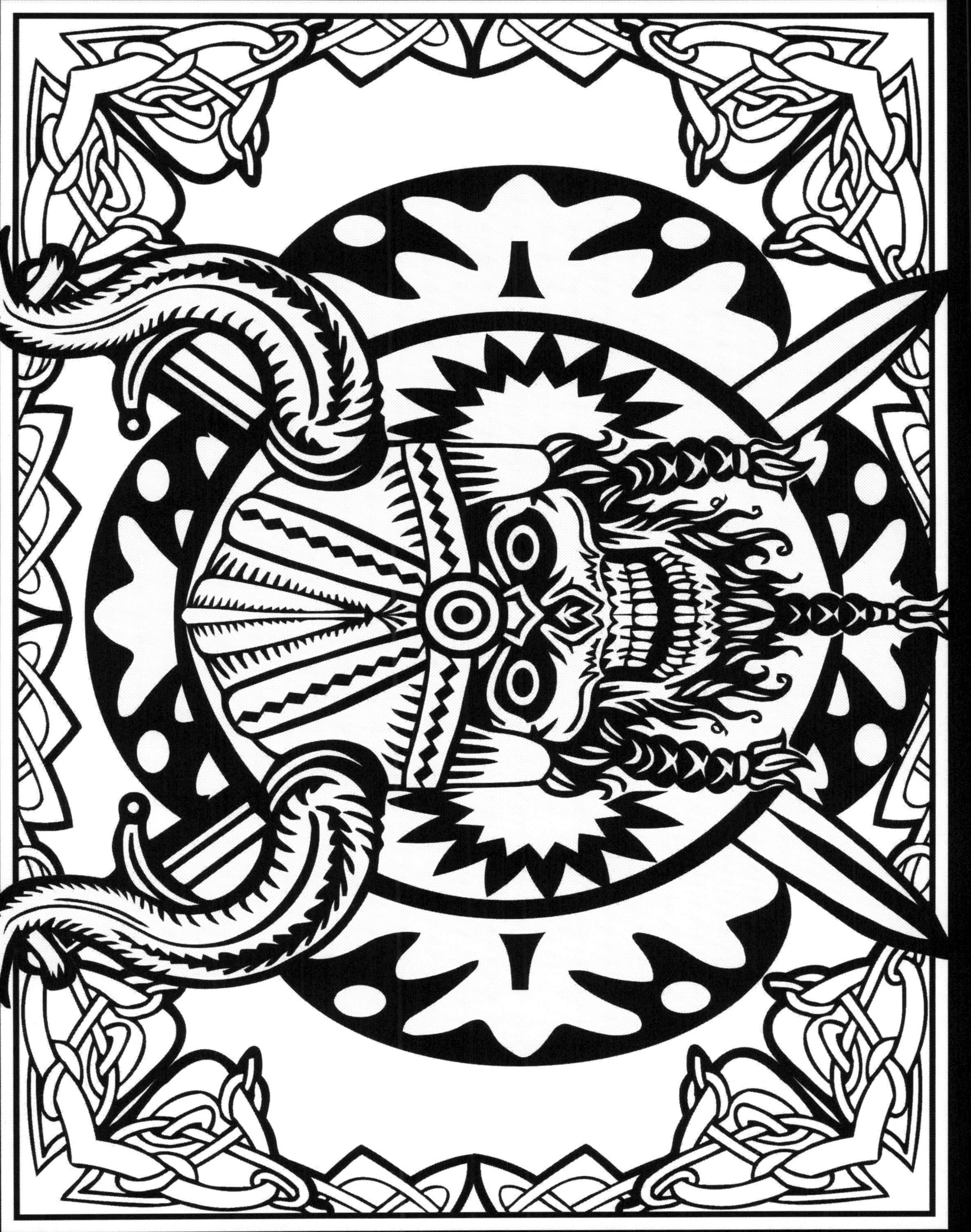

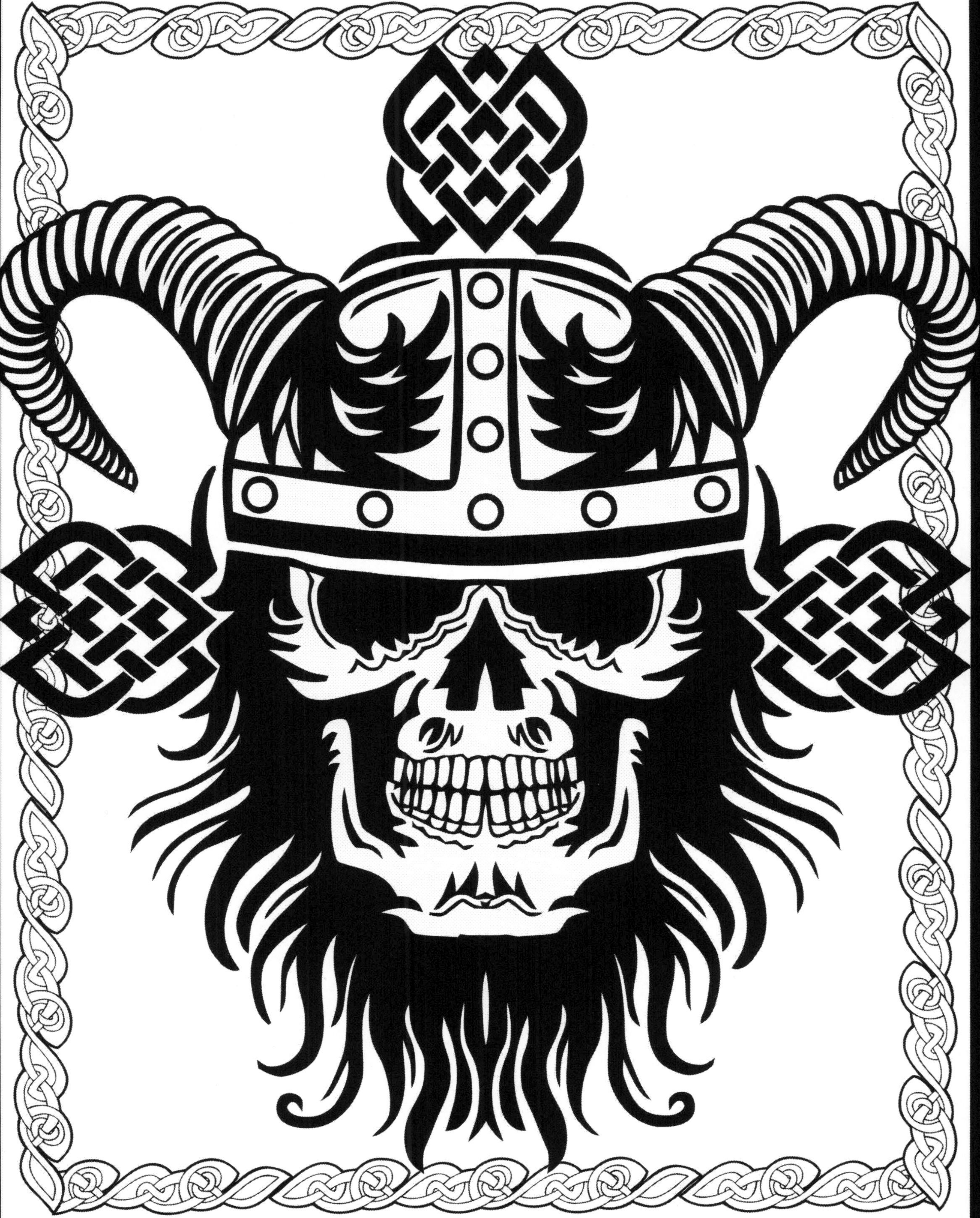

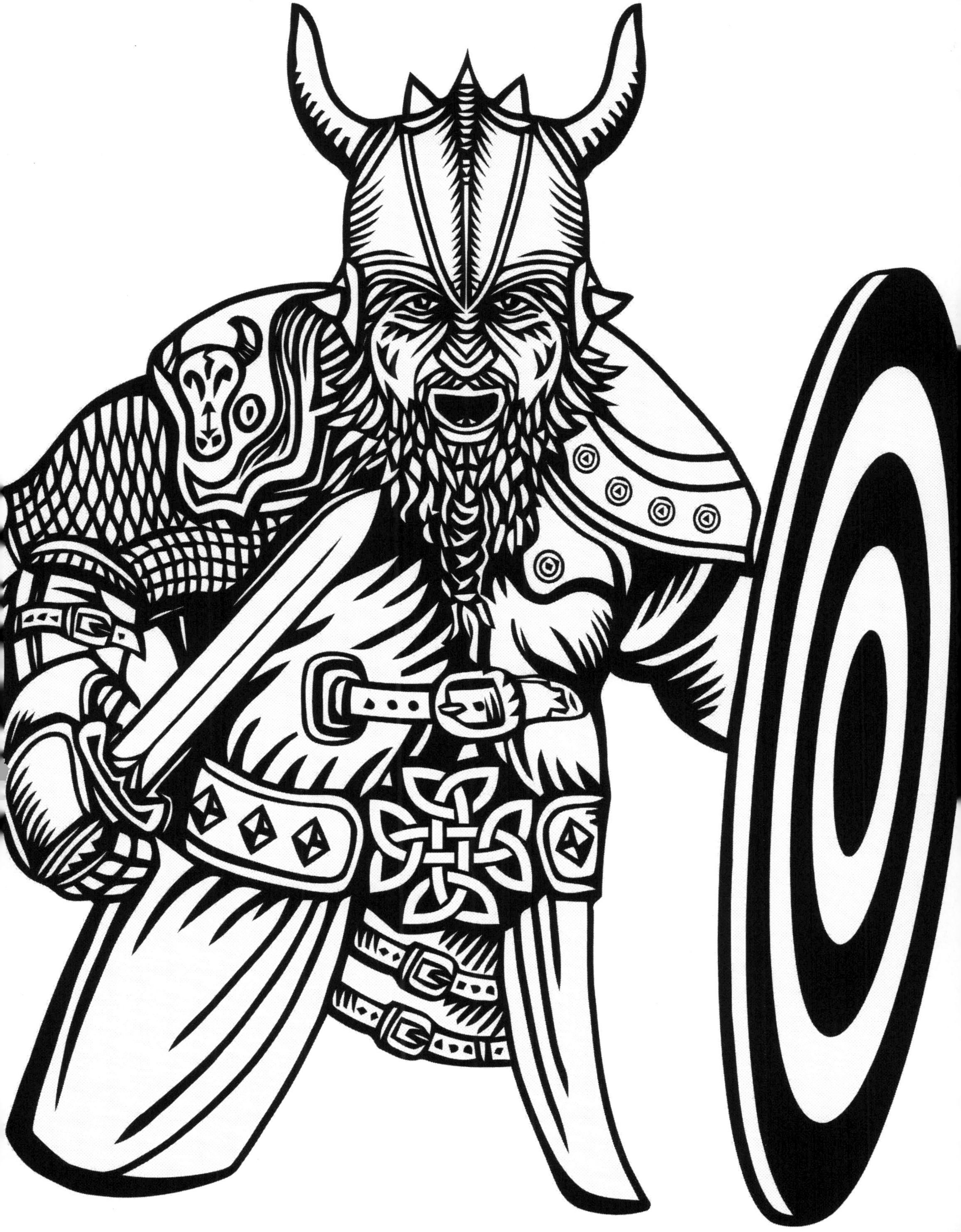

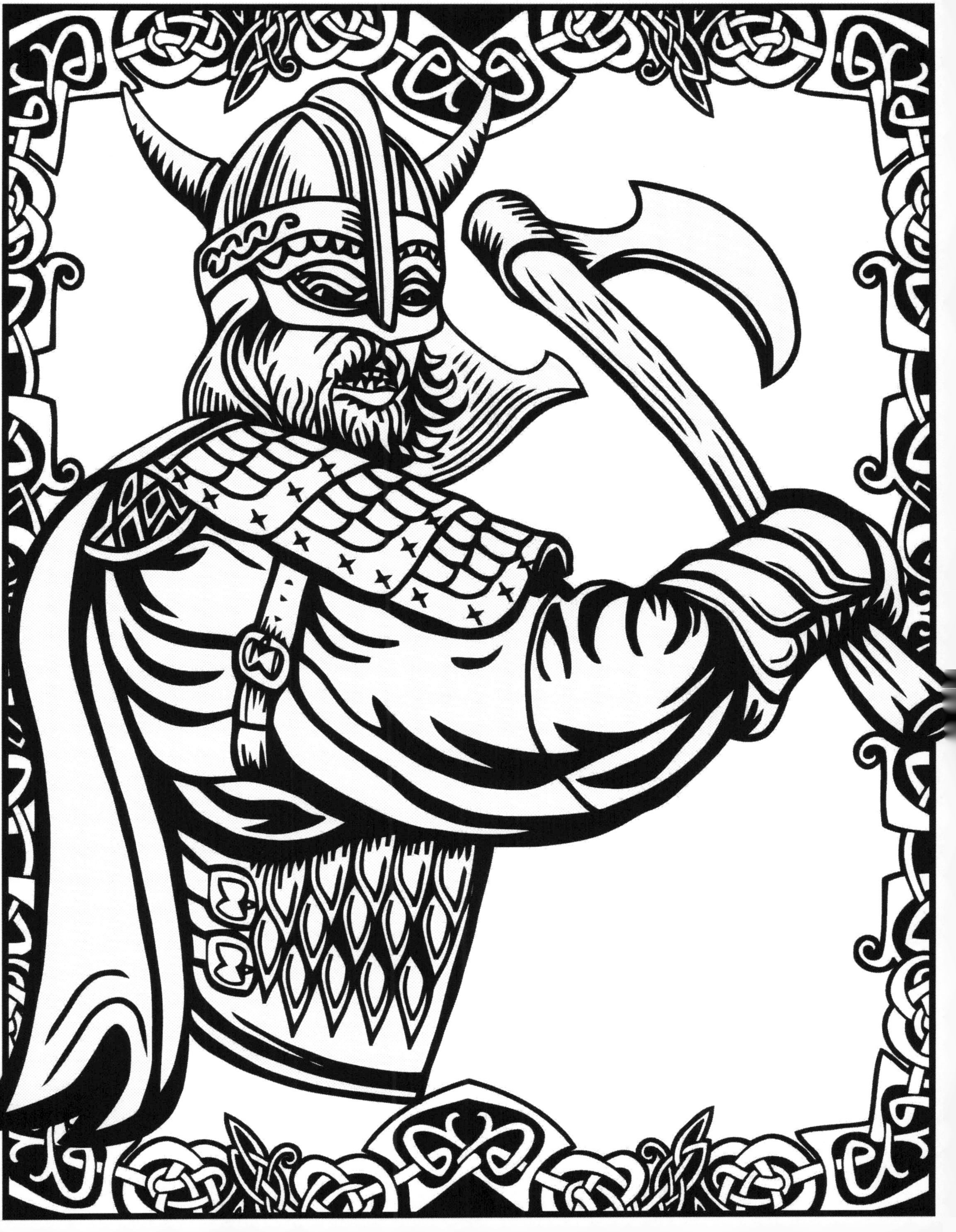

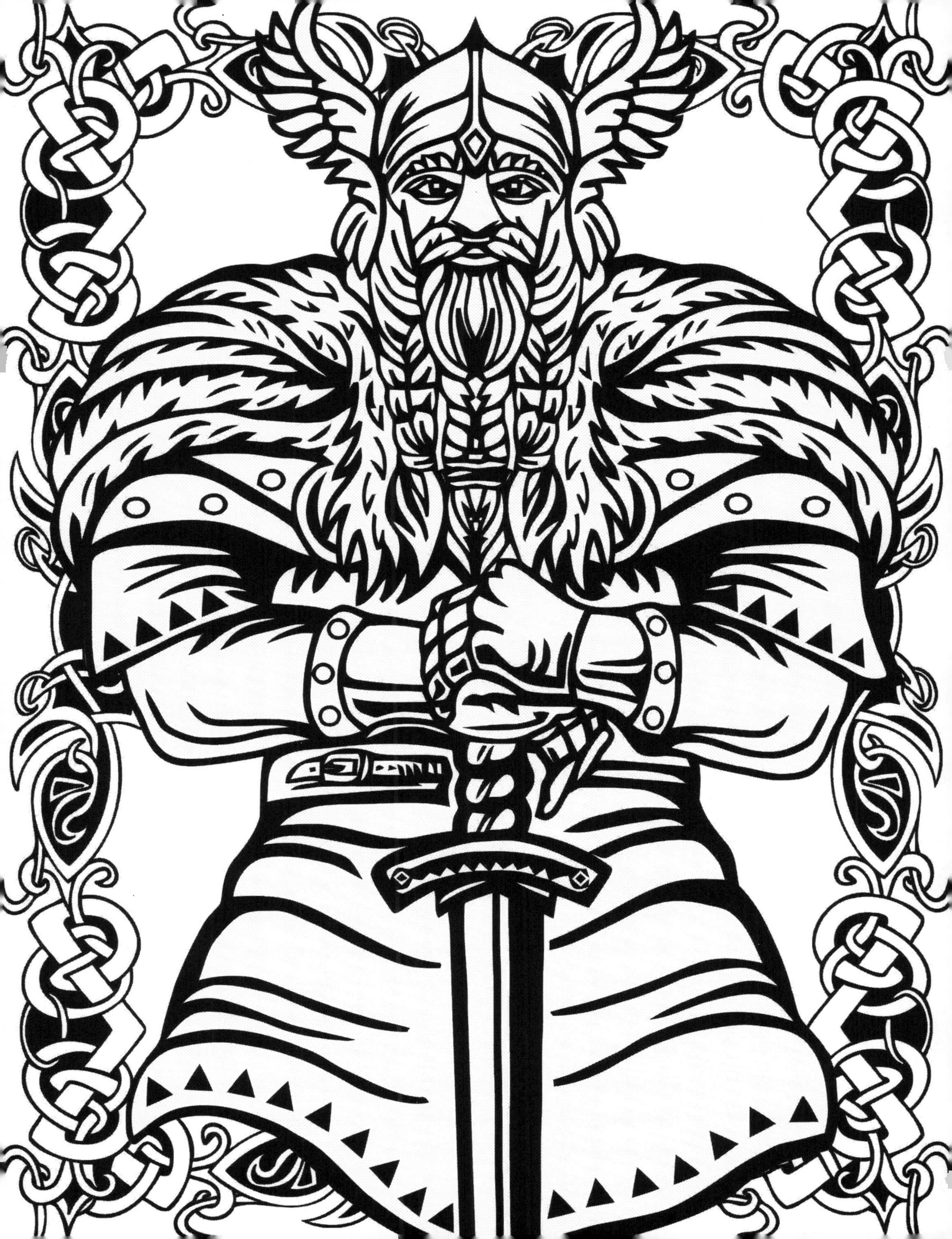

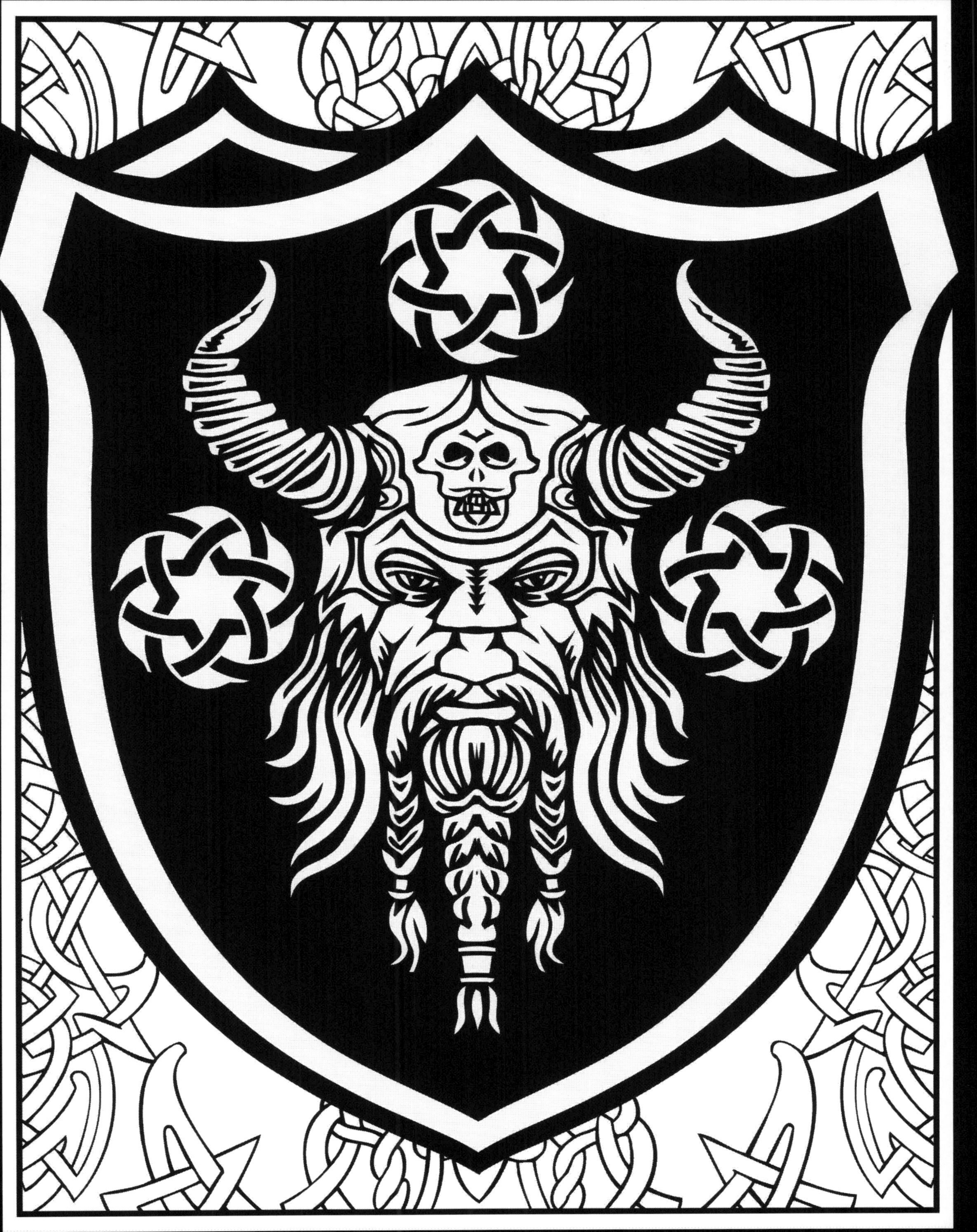

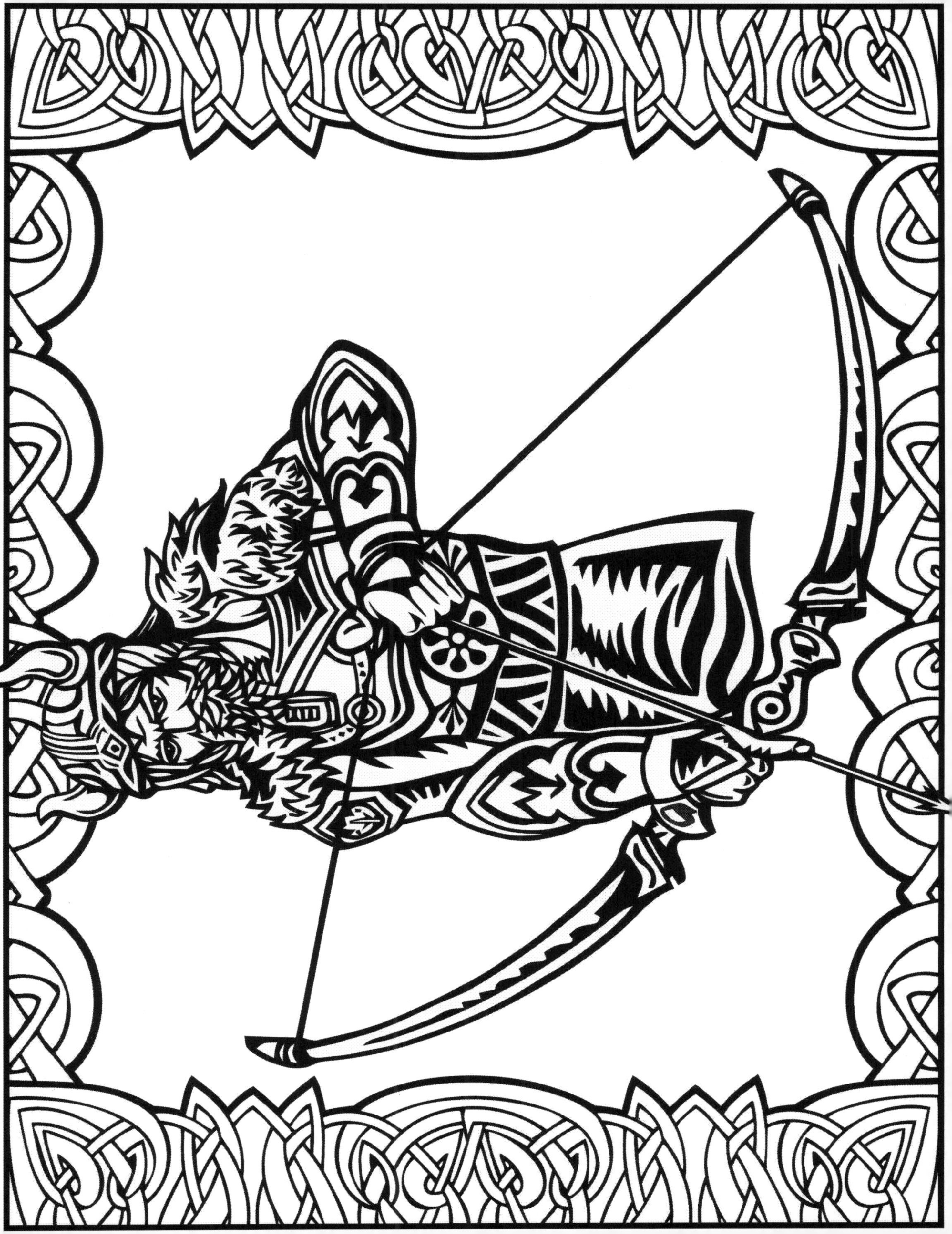

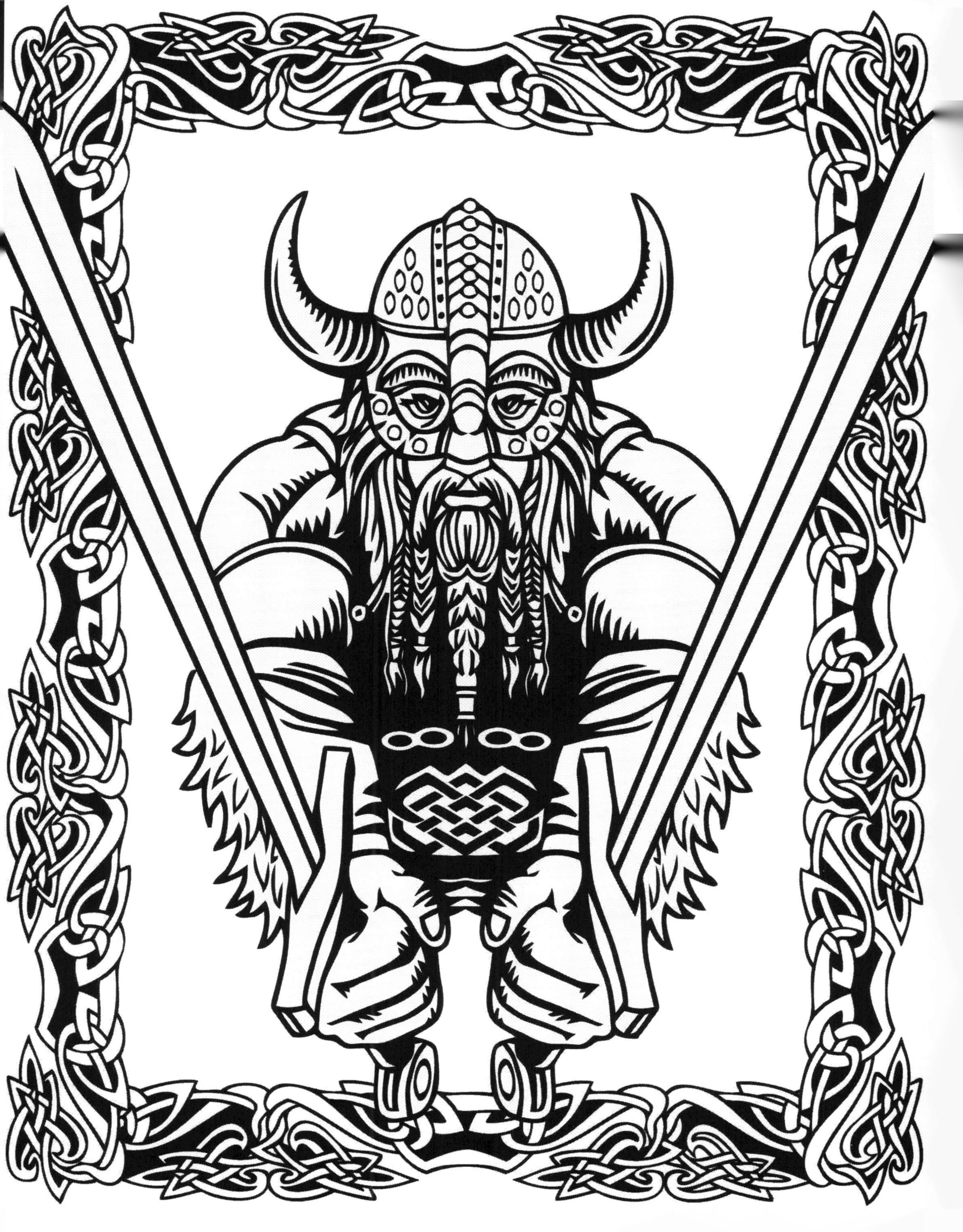

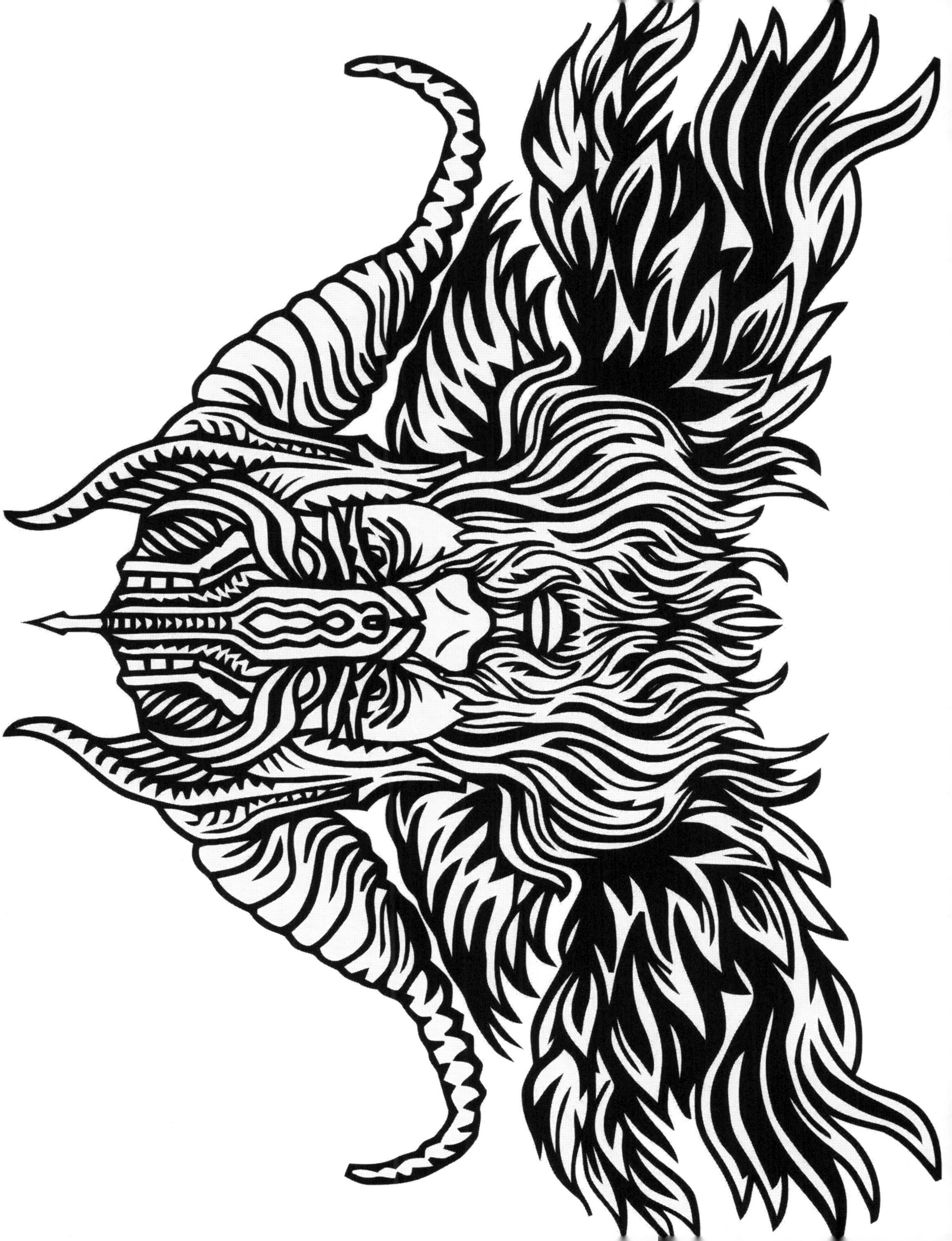

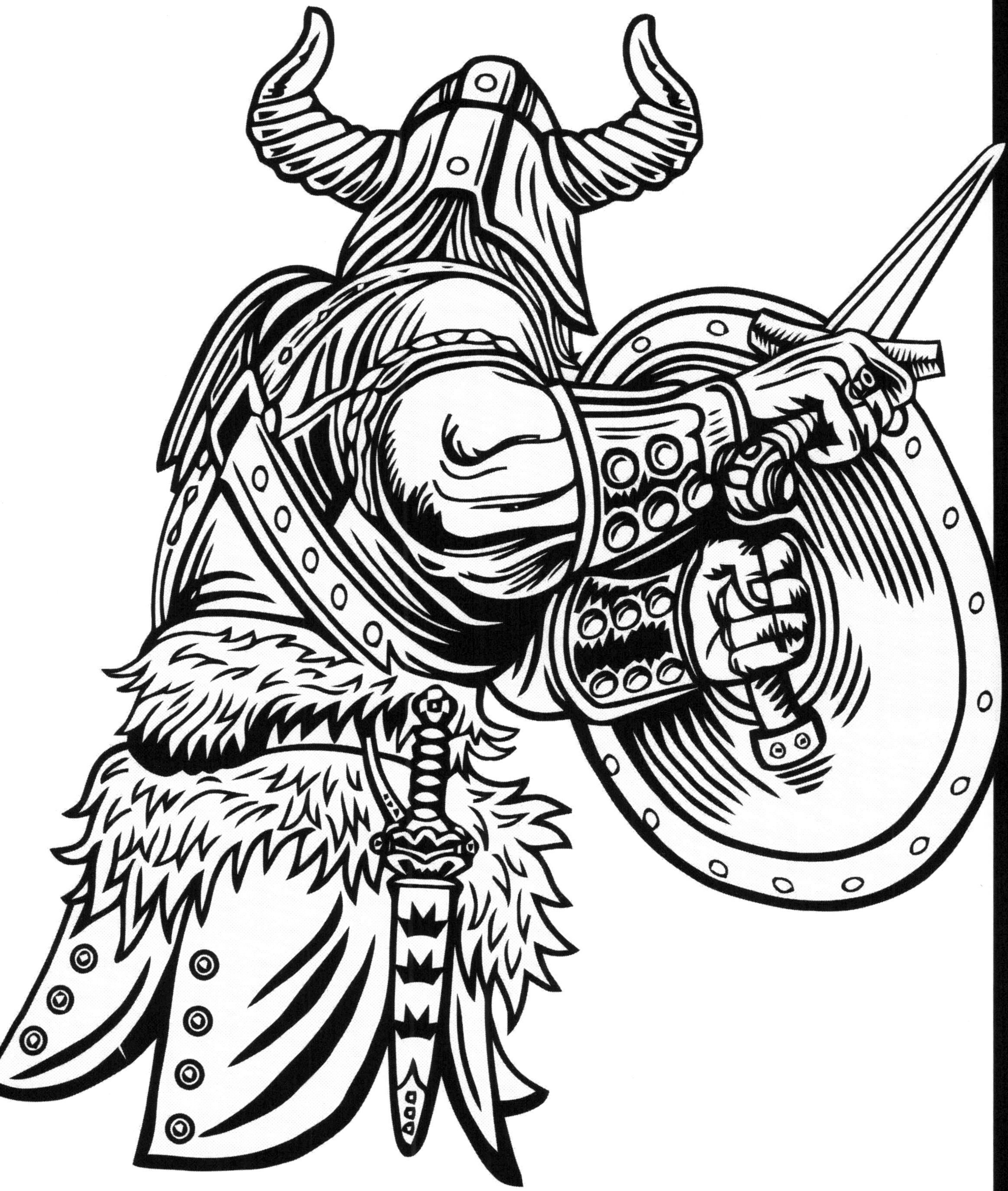

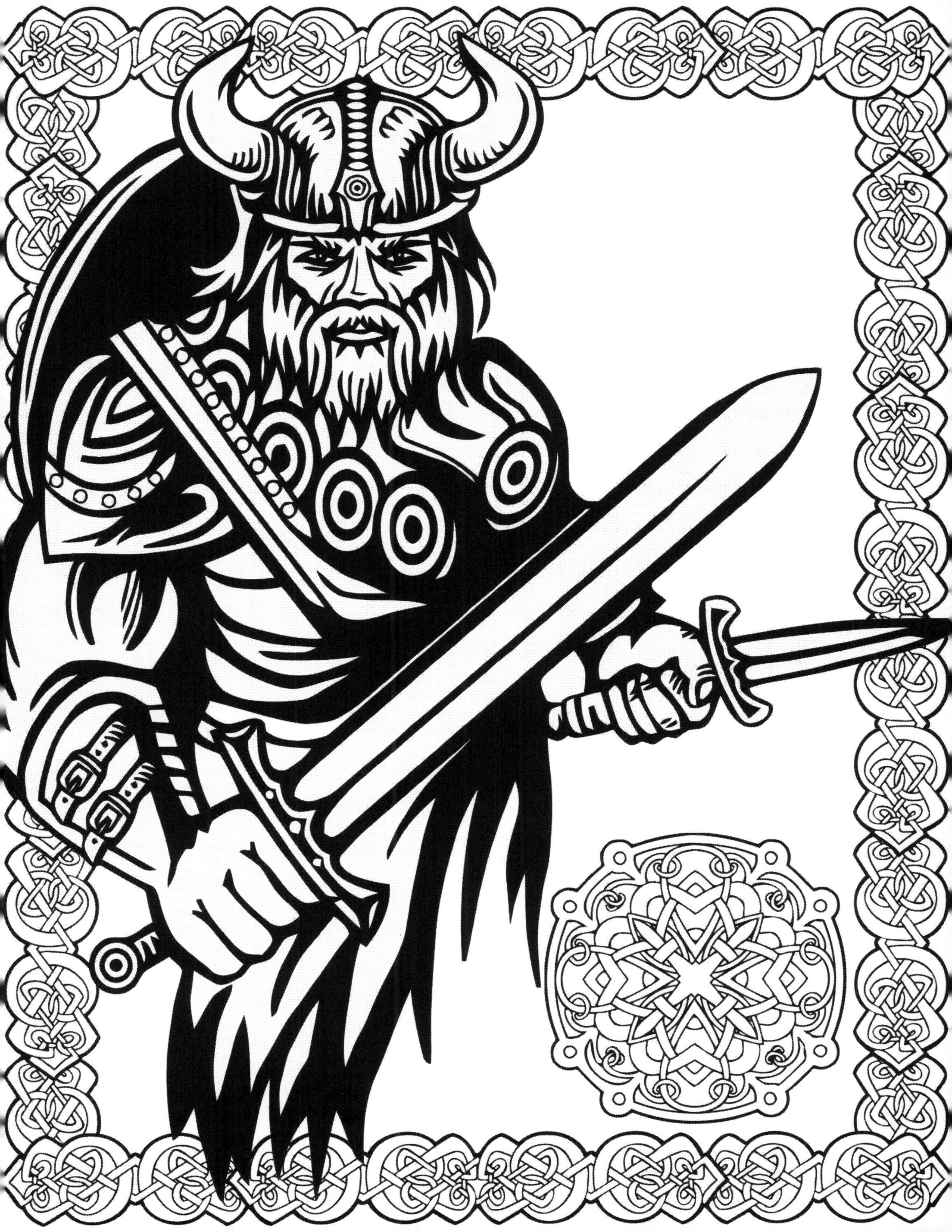

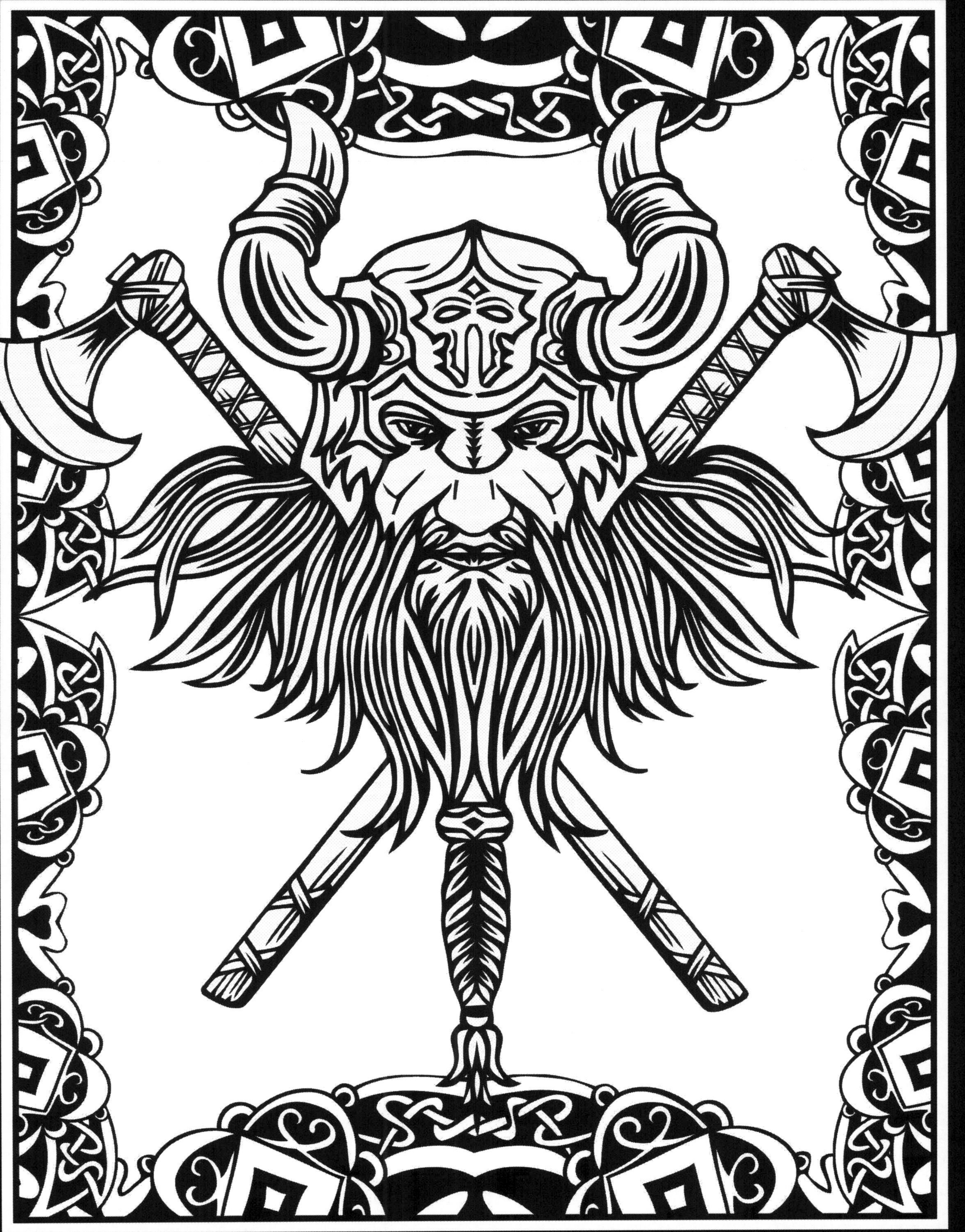

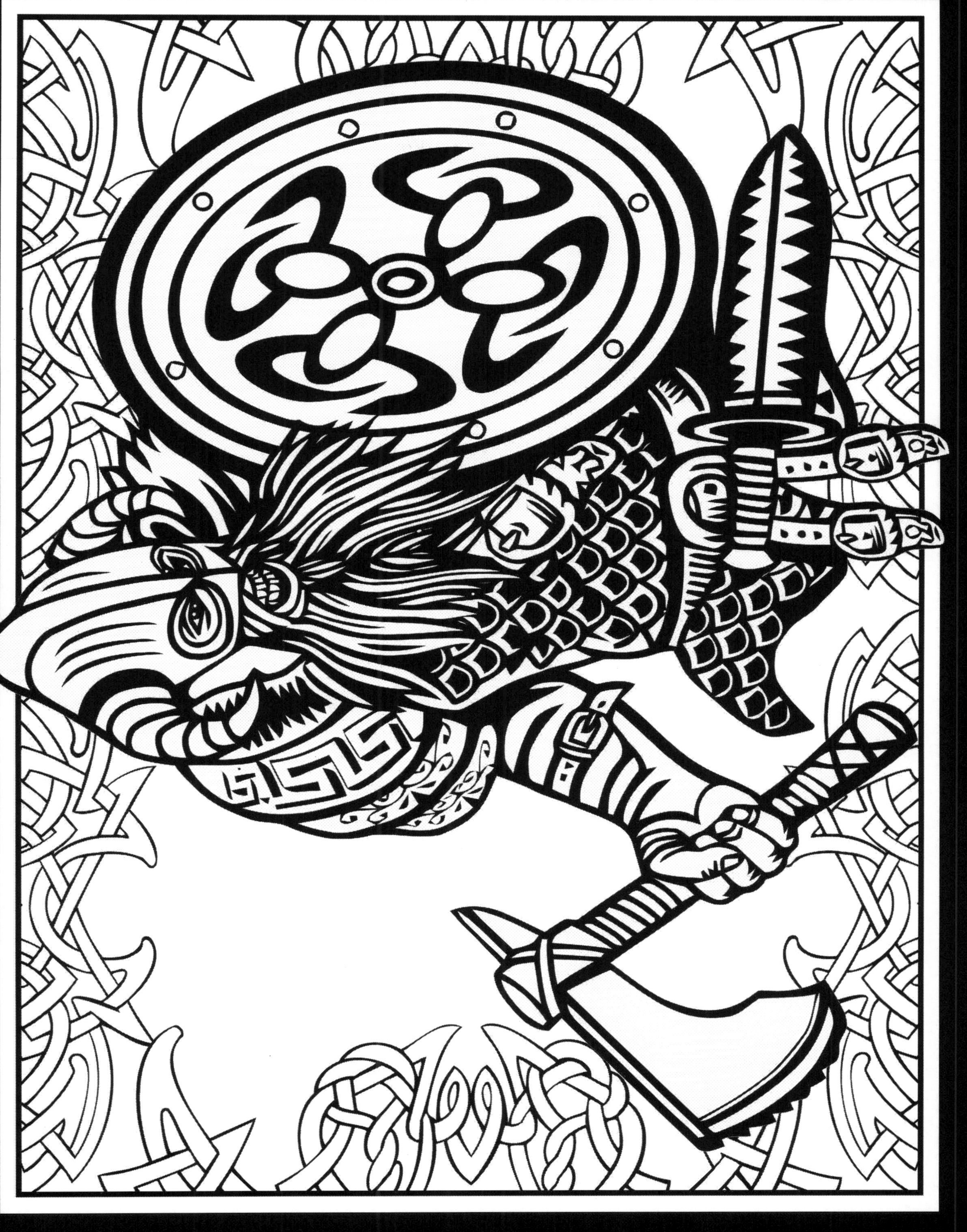

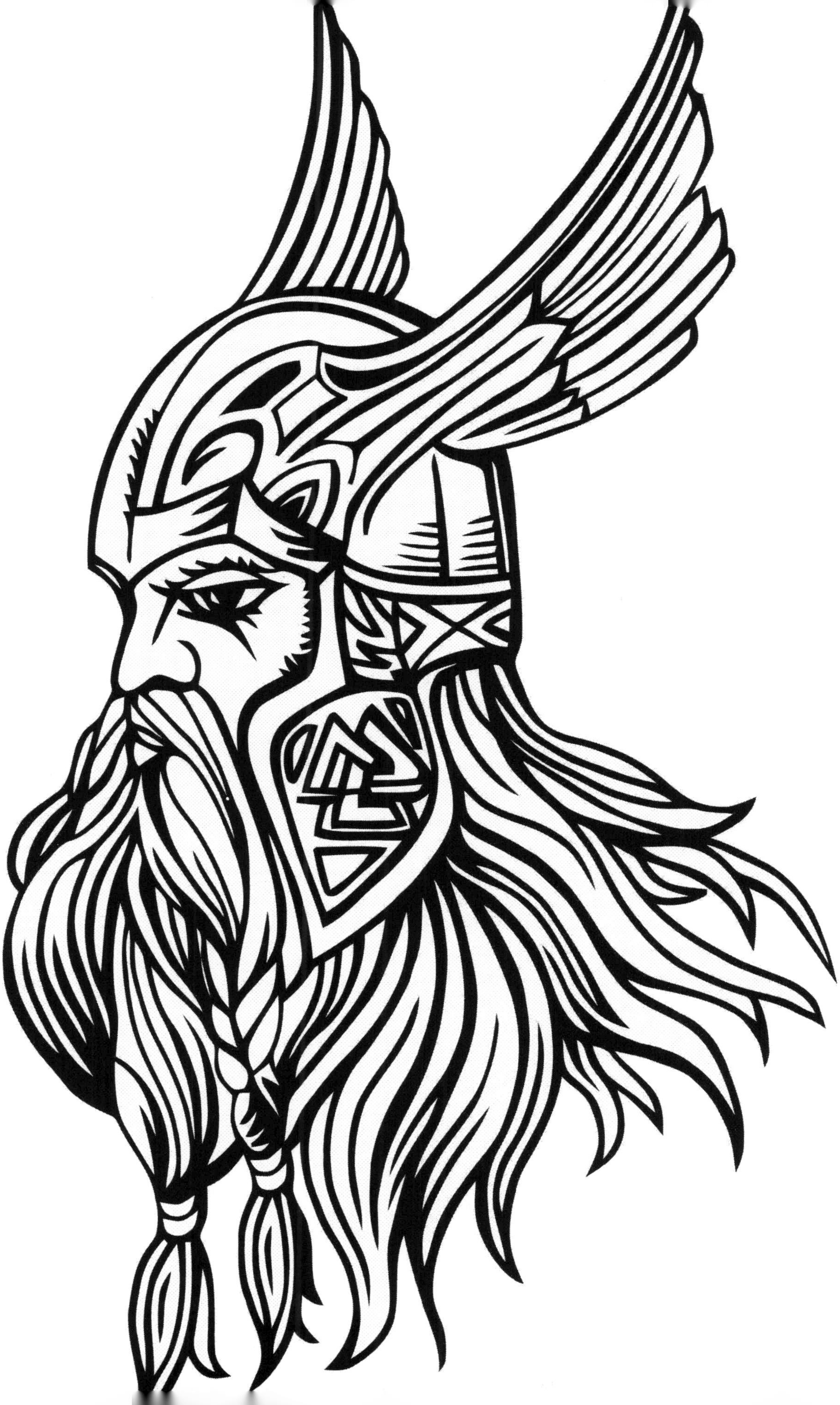

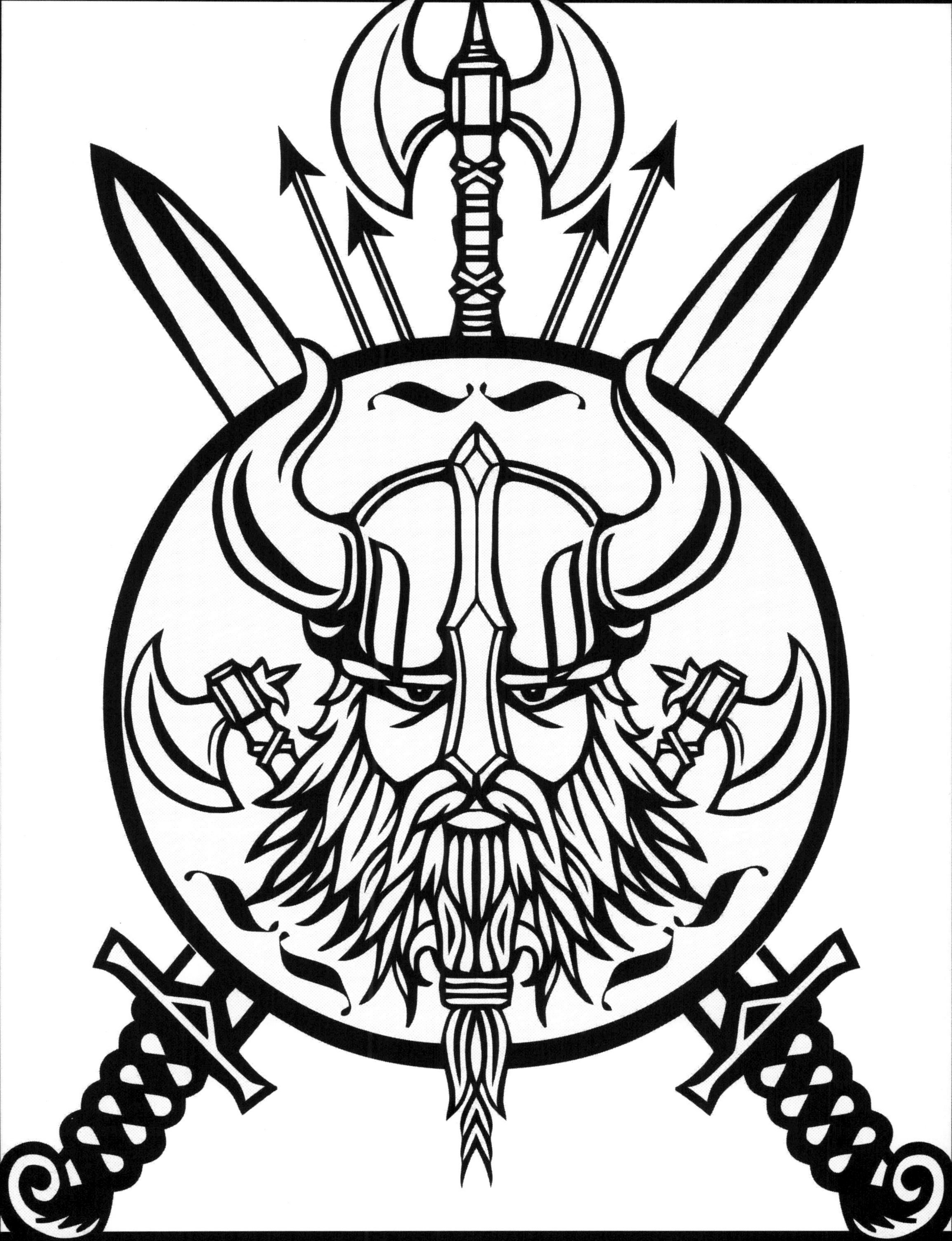

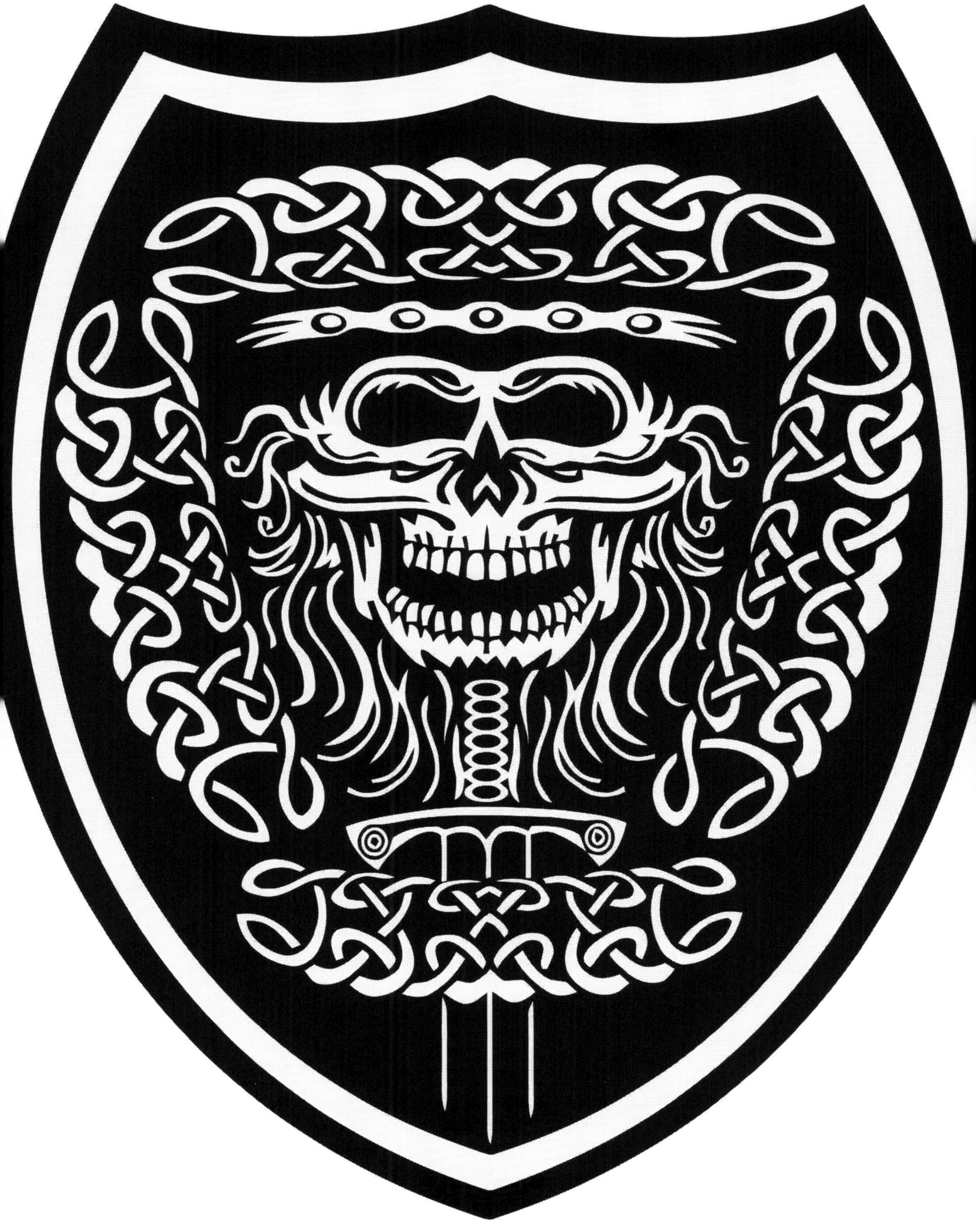

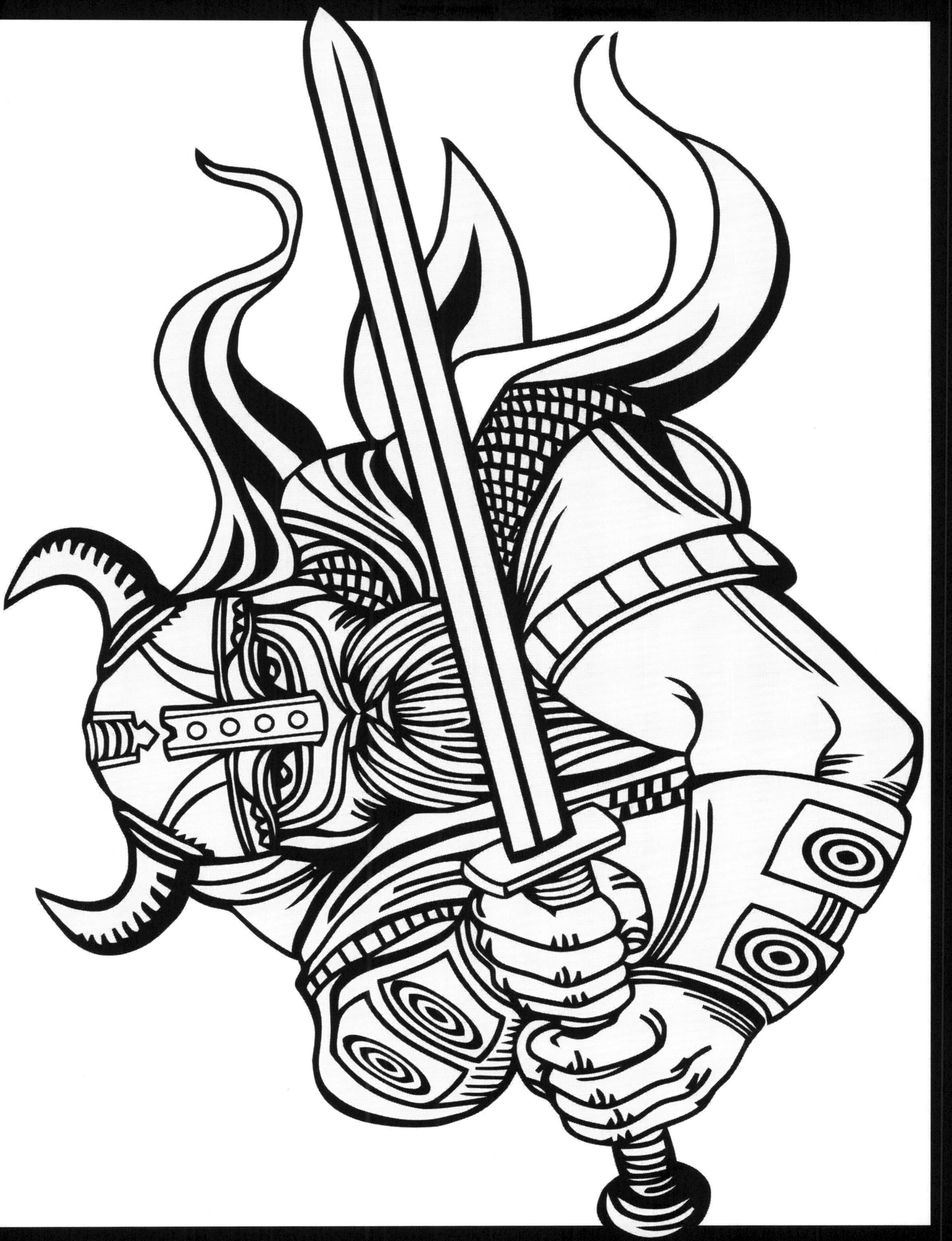

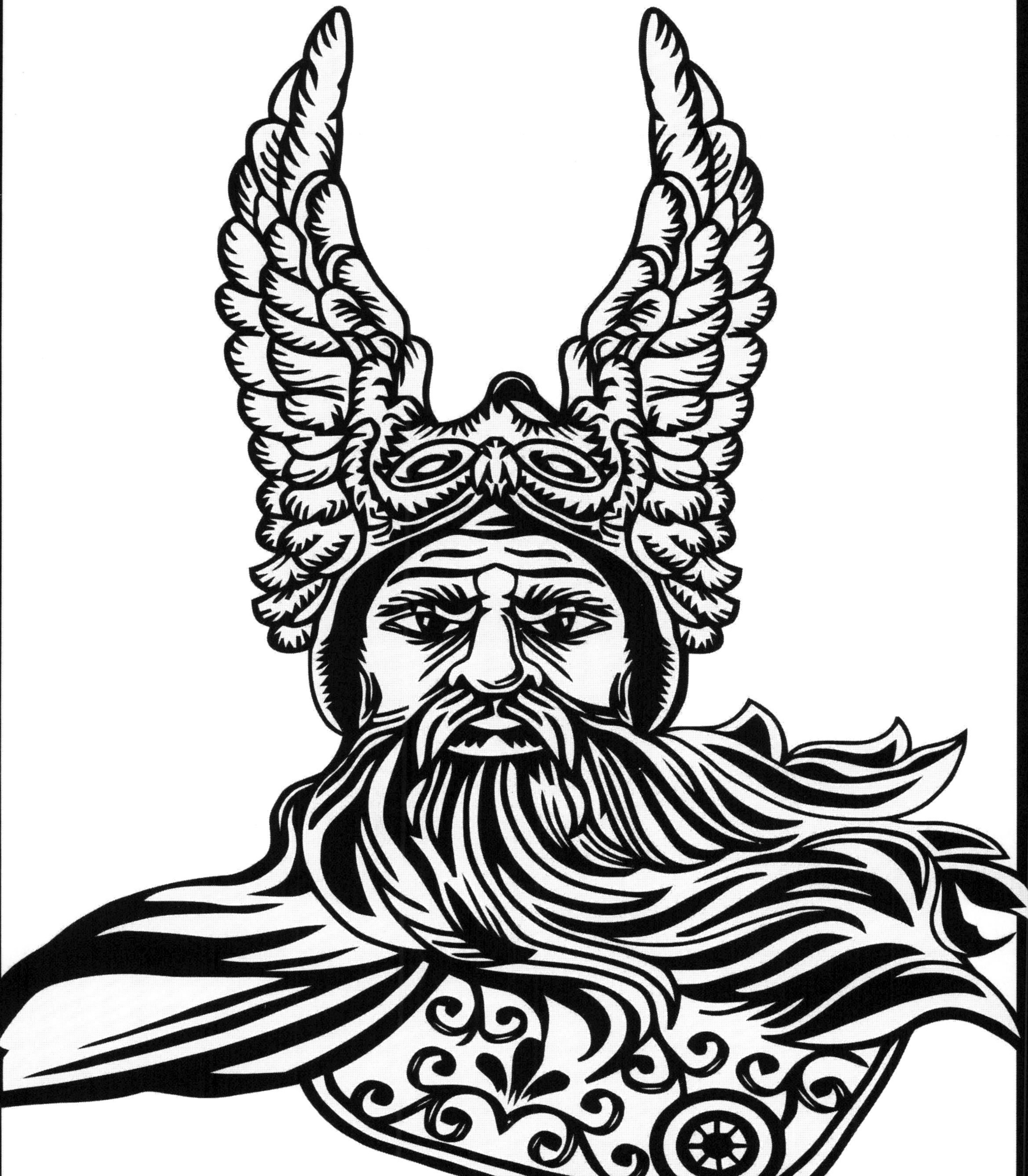

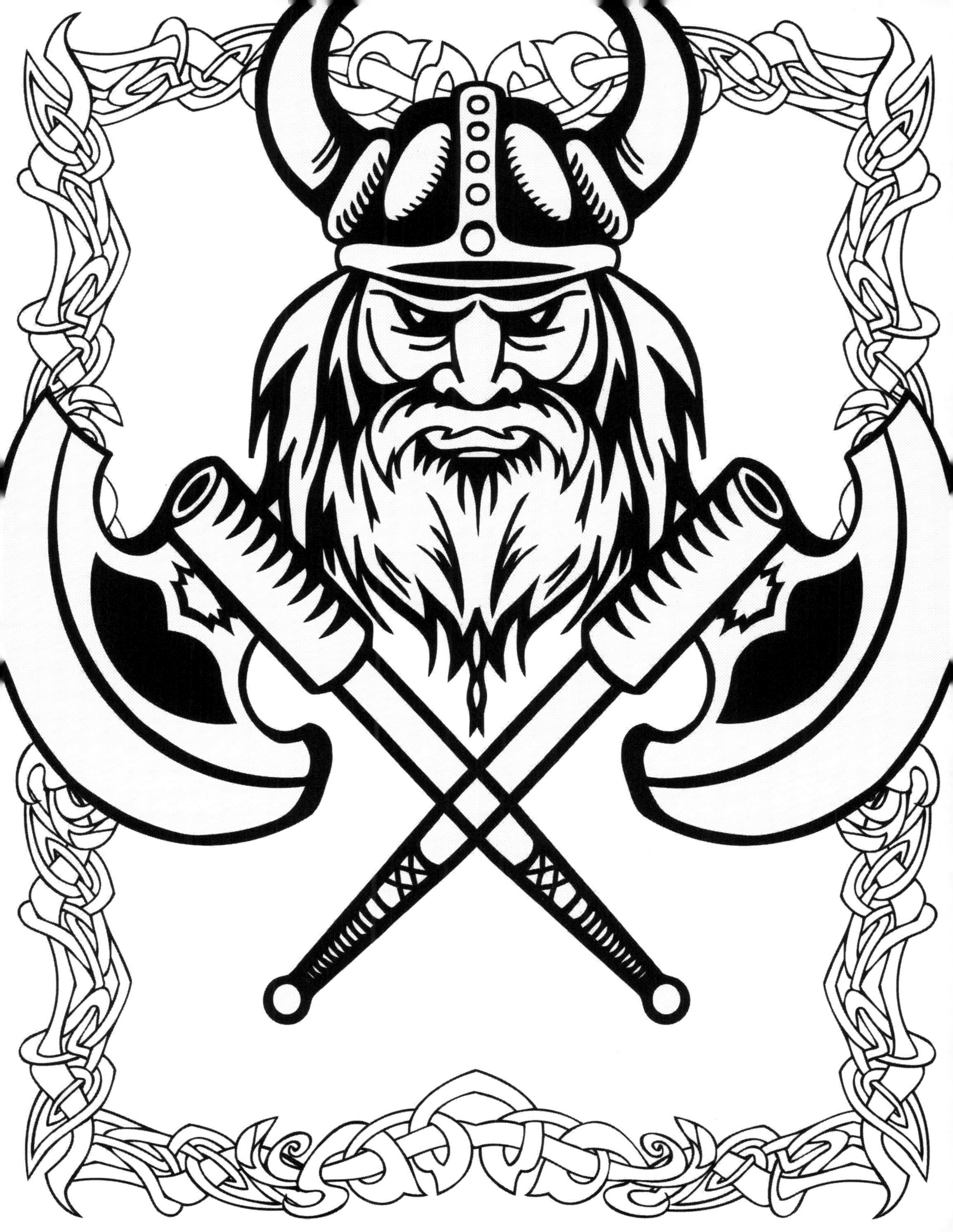

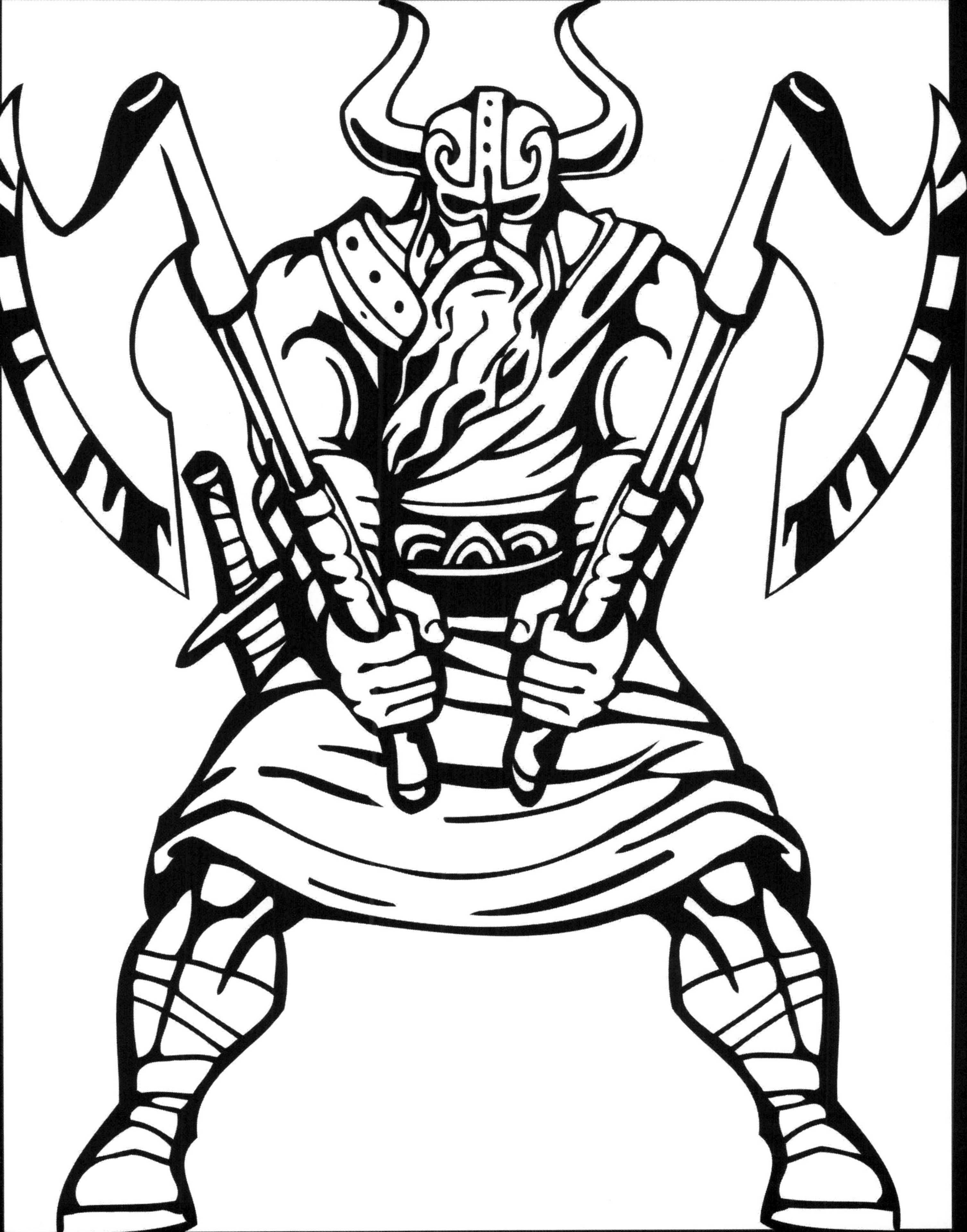

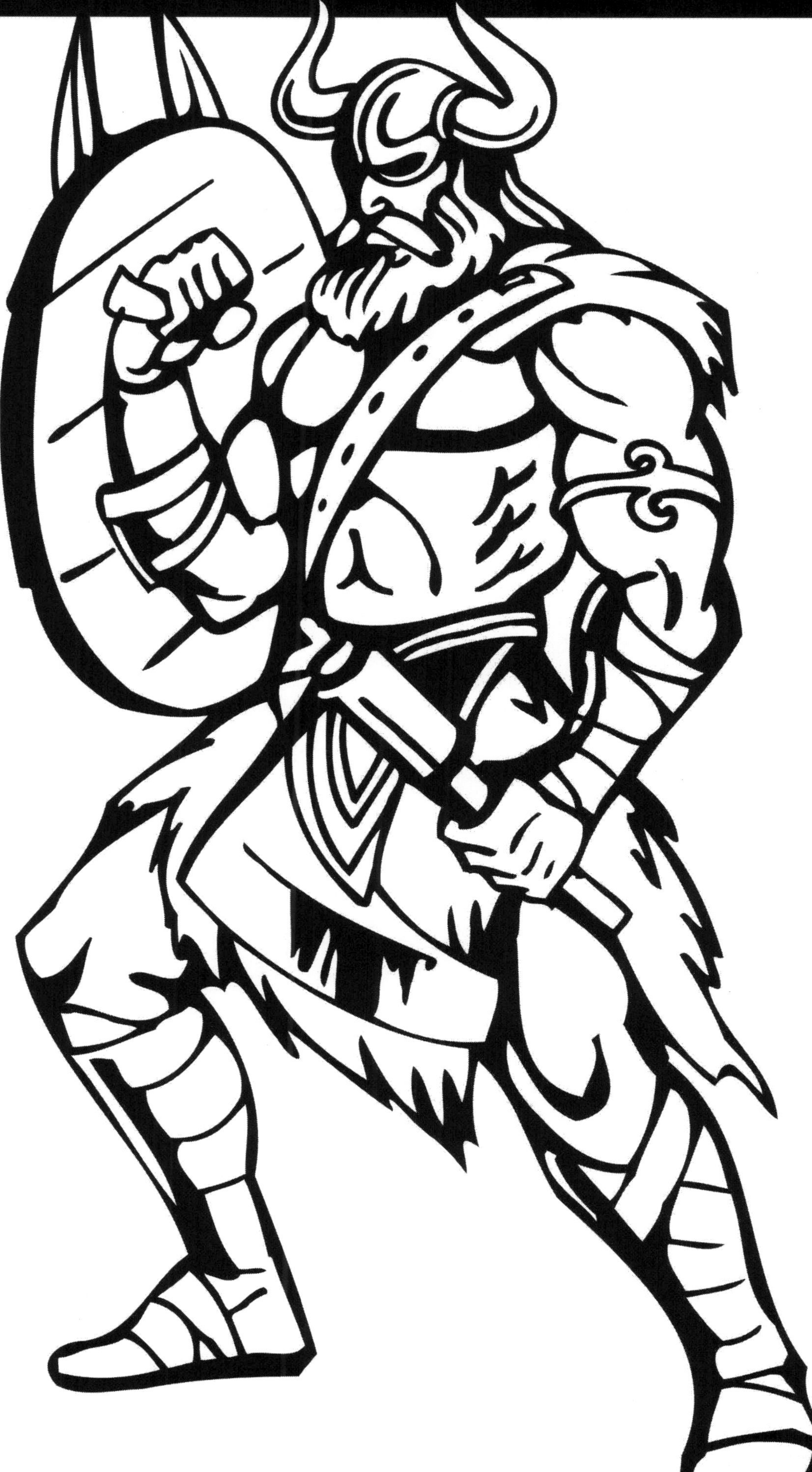

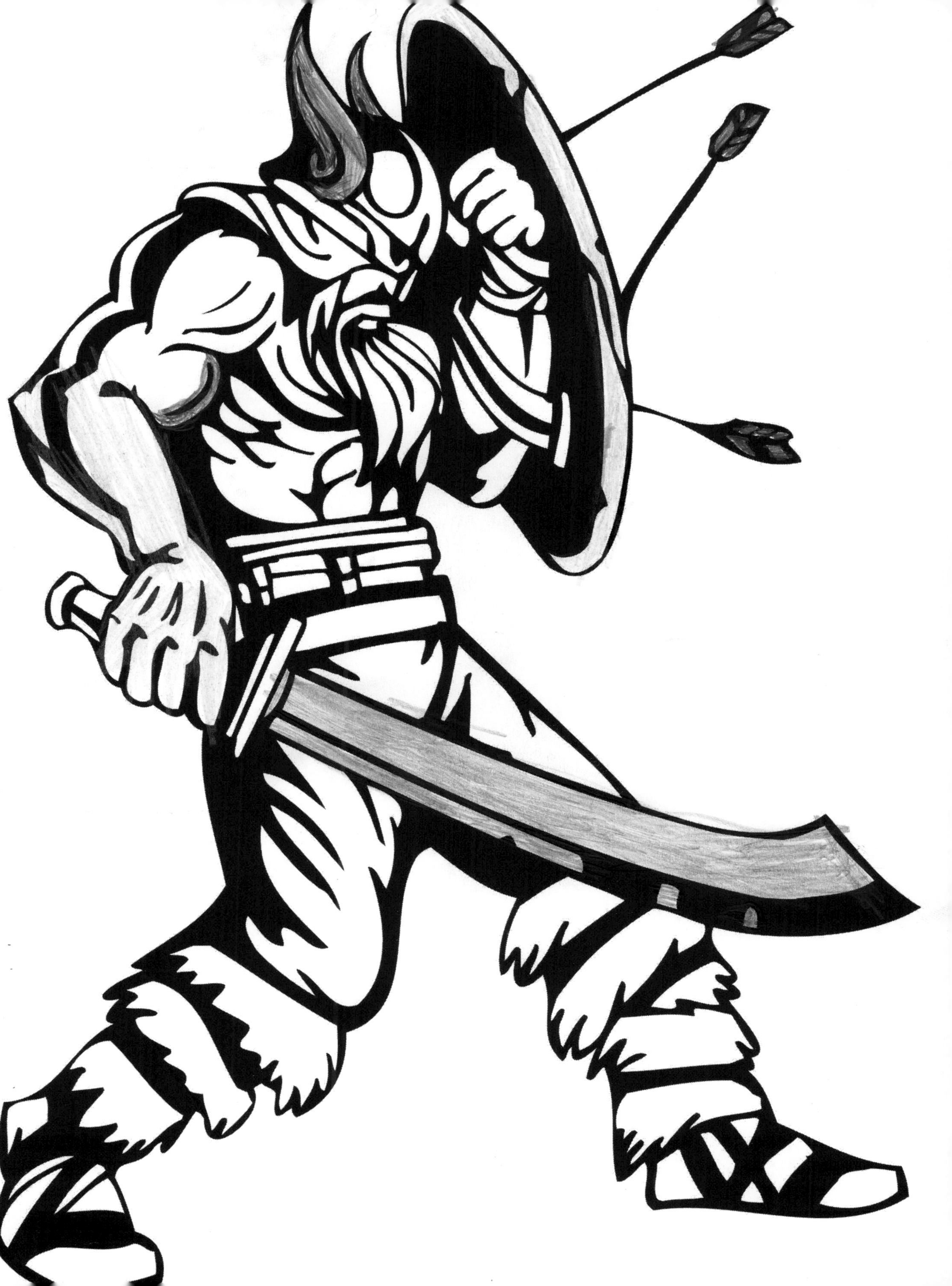

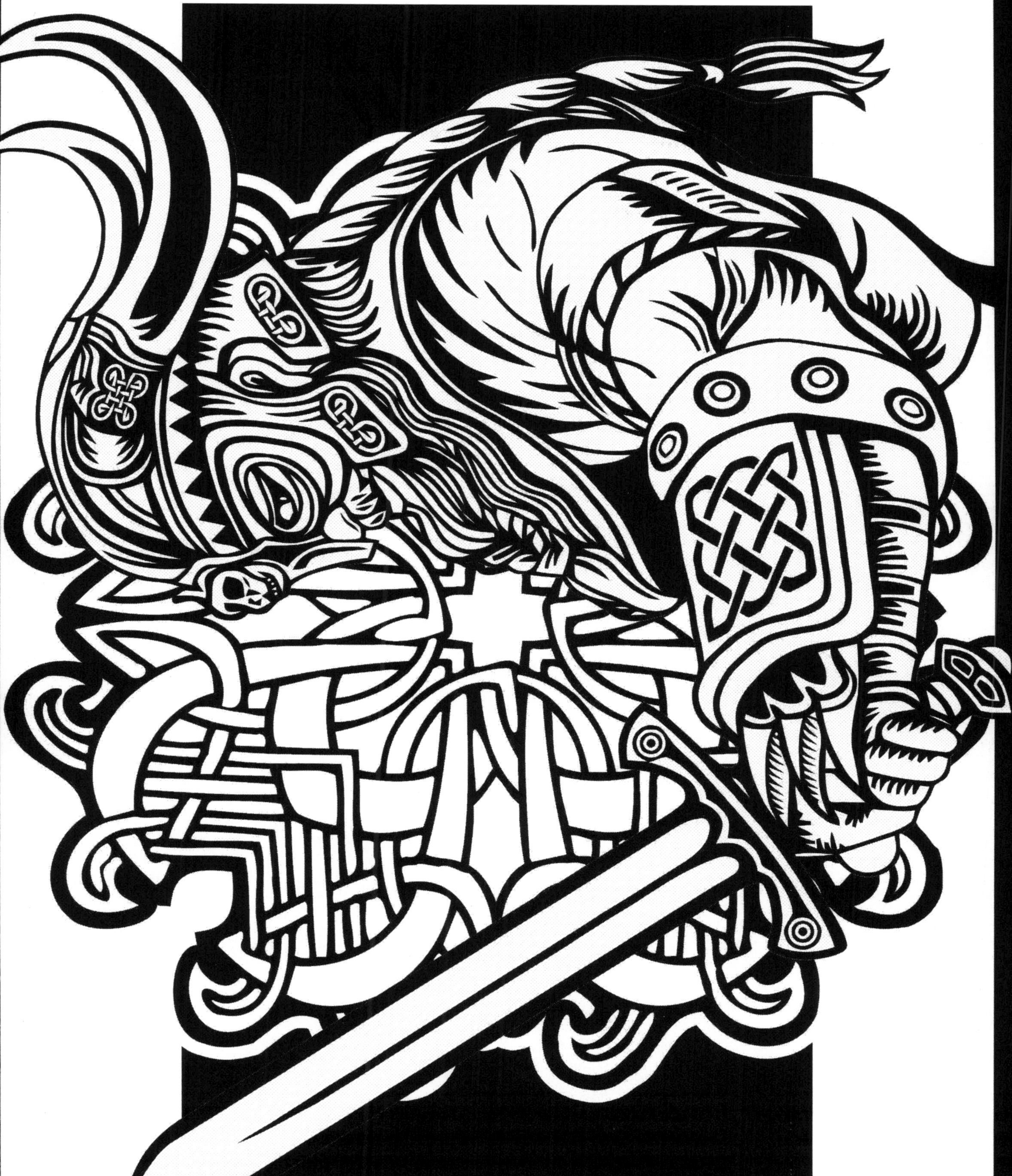

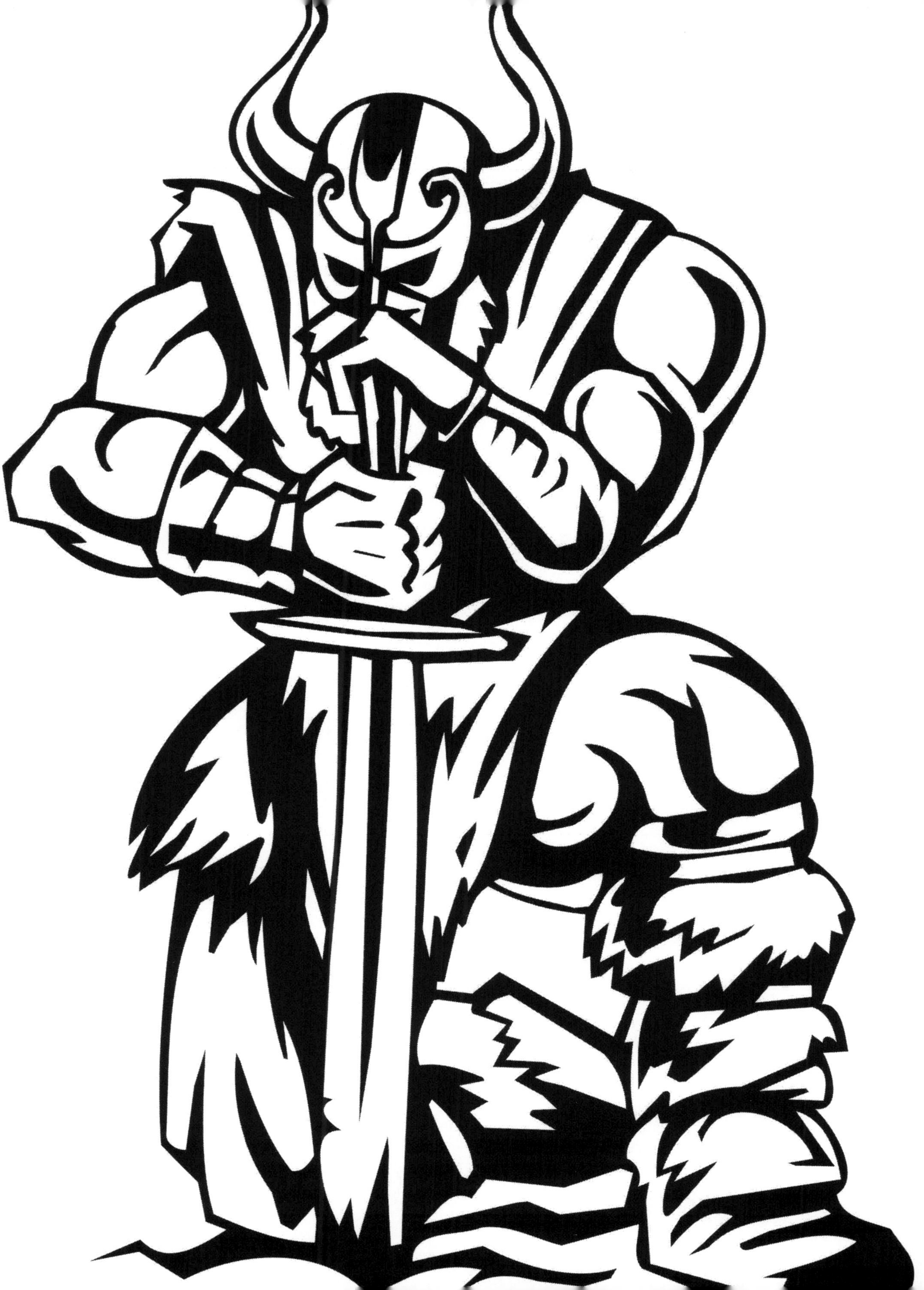

29954994R00059

Printed in Great
Britain
by Amazon